Journeys to
Self-Acceptance

Journeys to Self-Acceptance

FAT WOMEN SPEAK

Edited by Carol A. Wiley

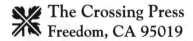

The Crossing Press
Freedom, CA 95019

Library of Congress Cataloging-in-Publication Data

Journeys to self-acceptance : fat women speak / [edited by] Carol A.
Wiley
       p. cm.
  Includes bibliographical references.
  ISBN 0-89594-657-2. -- ISBN 0-89594-656-4 (pbk.)
  1. Body image. 2. Self-acceptance. 3. Overweight women-
-Psychology. 4. Women--Psychology. I. Wiley, Carol A.
BF697.5.B63J68 1994
158'.1'082--dc20
                                      93-39815
                                        CIP

Contents

Carol A. Wiley

Introduction

Carol A. Wiley

Much has been written about body image, anorexia nervosa, bulimia, and how so many women think they are fat when they are not. But there's another viewpoint: women who *are* fat and must live in our thin-obsessed society. Fat women live with a continual barrage of negativity and diet propaganda from the media, the medical profession, and often friends and family. A 1992 commercial is typical. The commercial opens with a hectic household: kids running about noisily, woman busy in kitchen, and man on the telephone. Woman opens a diet soft drink. Man looks up from the telephone and asks, "Have you lost weight?" All the hectic activity falls away, triumphant music blares in the background, and woman grins as if she could receive no higher compliment.

The lie that losing weight will make a woman's life wonderful permeates our culture, but the women who wrote for this book have moved beyond this lie. Twenty-four women share their experiences, women who grew up fat and women who gained weight later in life, women moderately fat and women very fat. These women relate hurtful experiences from others, but even more poignantly, they relate how they internalized, then had to struggle to let go of, our culture's negative beliefs about fat. These essays show not only how difficult it is to be a fat woman in a thin culture but also the possibility and freedom of self-acceptance.

Growing up fat in America can be a harsh experience—from the taunts of other children to the pressure to lose weight exerted by adults. When I was in the seventh grade, I watched the teacher measure the height and weight of the other students then send them out to recess. I stepped on the scale: 5'7" and 214 pounds. The teacher had not wanted to embarrass me in front of the other children, yet her disapproval was obvious. All my life I had heard from adults that I should lose weight. All my life I had endured the taunts of other children: "Fatso," "Titanic." Two more years of this pressure and, at fourteen, I began fifteen years of yo-yo dieting, trying to fit my body into a package deemed acceptable by society.

Some women in this book speak of going on their first diet at age eight or ten; some spent far longer than my fifteen years trapped in what author Naomi Wolf refers to in *The Beauty Myth* as the "weight-loss cult." "Cult" seems an appropriate word for a situation where women voluntarily starve themselves. A "sensible" weight-loss diet contains 1200-1500 calories; many fad and very-low-calorie diets contain fewer. In comparison, during the Dutch famine of World War II, authorities maintained rations at a "semi-starvation" level of 600-1600 calories a day.

Our bodies don't know the difference between a famine and a diet and react to both by lowering metabolism to conserve energy. When food is again available, the body regains fat in preparation for the next famine. This biological mechanism is central to the oft-quoted ninety to ninety-five percent failure rate of diets. Yes, people lose weight, but most regain it, often gaining more than they lost, a fact recognized by the National Institutes of Health (NIH) at a spring 1992 conference on weight loss.[1] The NIH acknowledged that both low-calorie (1000-1500 calories) and very-low-calorie (less than 800 calories) diets may have adverse side effects, one of the most serious side effects of very-low-calorie diets being gallstones. In one study, twenty-five percent of the dieters on a 500-calorie-a-day diet developed gallstones within eight weeks compared to none of the "overweight" control group.

Even people who reach a lower weight may experience continuing side effects. One study by the Rockefeller Institute looked at women who had lost weight with Overeaters' Anonymous and were now at "normal" weight. The women had the symptoms of semi-starvation: shrunken fat cells, menstrual irregularities, abnormally low pulse rates, abnormally low blood pressure, and a constant feeling of being cold. These women also burned twenty-five percent fewer calories than their heights and weights indicated they should. To stay at "normal" weights, these women had to keep themselves half starved.

This finding is one of many that supports the setpoint theory: the body has a weight or range of weights to which it naturally gravitates. Even balanced low-calorie diets lead to chronic fatigue, impaired concentration, cold intolerance, and physical discomfort as body weight drops below its setpoint. Although the body's setpoint can change, it tends to stay the same. This setpoint, or natural weight, is largely inherited. Studies of adoptees have shown that their weights are more similar to their biological parents' than to their adopted parents'. This dispels the myth that fat parents make their children fat by teaching them inappropriate eating habits.

"The standard, 'sensible' recommendations to change eating habits and diligently use calorie charts are no more than elaborate folklore, expressions of faith in a world that ought to exist, but in fact does not," wrote William Bennett, M.D., and Joel Gurin in *The Dieter's Dilemma: Eating Less and Weighing More.*

Yet the diet mentality is ingrained. A 1989 study by MarketData Enterprises, a marketing research company, found that sixty-five million Americans diet every year, creating a thirty-three-billion-dollar-a-year diet industry, ranging from low-calorie sweeteners to commercial weight-loss programs. These programs are neither as safe nor as effective as advertised. In 1990 Congress held two days of hearings on the diet industry and heard testimony from people who had experienced ill effects on commercial weight-loss programs. Congress requested that the Federal Trade Commission (FTC) investigate industry practices. The FTC has reached consent agreements with some manufacturers of low-calorie liquid diets in which the manufacturers agreed to stop making weight loss and safety claims if they can't back them up with scientific evidence. The FTC continues to investigate other commercial weight-loss programs.

The Health Question

In any discussion of weight and fat, the question of health arises. Many myths are perpetuated about the effects of fat on health, based on flawed and incomplete studies. It all begins with those ubiquitous "desirable" weight tables, first published in the 1940s by the Metropolitan Life Insurance Company. These tables were based on long-term statistical studies (not a scientific, causal analysis) of life insurance policyholders. The studies showed a correlation between weight and death rates, but a closer look shows that the studies were seriously flawed.

First, the studies were sloppy. Applicants were weighed with their clothes and shoes, and only vague estimates were made about the effects of the apparel on weight and height. Some applicants reported their own weights and heights, and it has been found that people consistently underreport their weights. People were weighed only once, when they applied for insurance, so later weight changes were not considered.

Second, the participants did not represent the population as a whole. All participants were buying life insurance, an uncommon practice at the time, which probably meant they had higher than average incomes and often worked in safe occupations. Most were of Northern European ancestry, a group that tends to be taller and leaner than other ethnic groups.

Third, the studies did not consider age, even though cross-culturally most people gain weight as they get older.

Several authors have concluded that after you expose the fallacies of the insurance studies, all they prove is that older people die more often than younger people. Bennett and Gurin conclude, "'Desirable' weight is a statistical fiction." Data from other studies lead to the conclusion that the thinnest and heaviest people have the highest death rates, but that finding leaves a wide range of healthy weights.

Even the statement of the 1992 NIH conference said, "The evidence that reductions in mortality follow weight loss is meager." Bennett and Gurin point out that as the average weight of Americans has risen since

1965, heart disease has decreased and expected lifespan has increased. Further evidence of the exaggerated effects of fat can be found in "Rethinking Obesity: An Alternative View of its Health Implications" from *The Journal of Obesity and Weight Reduction*. Doctors Paul Ernsberger and Paul Haskew examined numerous studies and drew these conclusions:

- Women with weights associated with maximum longevity are considerably overweight by medical standards.
- Longstanding leanness is possibly a predisposing factor for cancer. Both lung and stomach cancer occur less often in fat people.
- Increased estrogen produced by fat protects against osteoporosis (a more recent study showed that dieting increases the risk of osteoporosis).
- Serious obstetric complications are less common in fat mothers than in lean ones.
- Fat people are more likely to survive heart disease. Atherosclerosis is entirely unrelated to body fatness. Losing and regaining weight may cause cardiovascular disease and death.
- Excess muscle is possibly more hazardous than excess fat.

Diabetes is a disease often associated with fat, but some indications suggest people do not get diabetes because they are fat but they are fat because they are predisposed to diabetes. Type II, adult-onset, diabetes develops because the body does not respond to the insulin secreted to lower blood sugar. Because the body is not responding, more insulin is produced. Insulin promotes the accumulation of fat. More fat, in turn, further increases insulin production. Some people stabilize at a certain insulin and fat level; others do not and become diabetic. Weight reduction can help some people control their diabetes but does not guarantee benefits: One study of 135 "overweight" Type II diabetics found that less than half (fifty-five) of them benefited from weight loss.[2] Exercise also can help control diabetes, even without weight loss.

Weight reduction is also generally believed to lower blood pressure, but again it may not benefit everyone. One study concluded, "At best, weight loss offers very limited benefit for overweight hypertensives. At worst, weight loss programs are expensive to run, cause considerable patient discomfort and may delay the implementation of more effective therapy."[3]

Many studies have shown that being heavy has some benefits and that the composition of the diet is more important than body weight. No disease affects fat people that does not also affect thin people. Fat may protect a person from some diseases and predispose her to others, so why should we conclude that "fat" diseases are worse than "thin" diseases? We might conclude, as Bennett and Gurin do, "The medical condemnation of obesity has been based more on emotion than on evidence."

A factor often ignored in studies of fat and health is stress. Stress results in the secretion of hormones that lower the body's immunity and increase the production of insulin. Living with prejudice and discrimination, as fat people often do, is very stressful. Dieting is also very stressful, especially the common yo-yo dieting—continually losing and regaining weight— which places far more stress on the body than extra pounds.

The Psychological Question

A persistent myth is that fat people necessarily have emotional problems or are compulsive overeaters. The American Psychiatric Association does not agree. The 1980 edition of the *Diagnostic and Statistical Manual of Mental Disorders* states, "Simple obesity is . . . not generally associated with any distinct psychological or behavioral syndrome." In fact, emotional problems may more often be the result of dieting.

If we reinterpret fat people as chronic dieters and look at dieting behavior, we see a different picture. Extensive research by Janet Polivy and C. Peter Herman of the University of Toronto with restrained and unrestrained eaters supports this reinterpretation. Restrained eaters (dieters) force themselves to eat less than they want while unrestrained eaters eat according to their bodies' signals. Polivy's and Herman's studies show that characteristics often associated with fat people are actually characteristics of restrained eaters (dieters) of any weight. The studies include these results:

- Dieters do not respond normally to a full or empty stomach; they eat in reaction to external cues. That is, dieting requires that a person ignore internal hunger cues, breaking the usual relation between hunger and eating.
- Dieters have an exaggerated preference for sweets and good-tasting foods.
- Dieters, but not nondieters, eat differently around people than when alone.
- Dieters are more emotional than nondieters, a finding that Polivy and Herman attribute to the constant stress imposed by dieting.
- Dieters are more easily distracted and more tied to the environment than nondieters.
- When dieters feel they have broken their diet, they exhibit what Polivy and Herman call the "what-the-hell-effect" and eat more, regardless of how much they have already eaten.

Polivy and Herman note that chronic dieting is now the norm, but that "it requires behaviors and attitudes that are self-destructive and pathological."[4] They conducted a clinical study of what they call "undieting," where they taught people to eat according to their bodies' signals. They concluded that a clinical program that helps people stop putting energy into fruitless attempts to lose weight could improve lives.[5]

Where We Are

Even as more people acknowledge the biological basis of weight and the futility of dieting, an emerging view of obesity as a chronic disease to be treated like high blood pressure or diabetes is not encouraging. In October 1992, the *New York Times* reported that diet pills, long out of favor with doctors, were again gaining favor as a long-term medication after a study showed the pills help people lose weight and keep it off *as long as they continue taking the pills*. Possible side effects of these pills include sleep disorders, increased blood pressure, depression, diarrhea, headaches, and stomach disturbances.

This desire for drugs is distressing. Will we ever become more tolerant of human variety? Perhaps Marcia Germaine Hutchinson is right when she writes in *Transforming Body Image*, "When enough people change their consciousness to embrace a new set of values, the values of their culture will change." The perception of fat is changing, slowly. A size-acceptance movement is spreading across America. The National Association to Advance Fat Acceptance (NAAFA) works to educate people and to support fat people fighting discrimination. I hope this book will help change perceptions.

My perceptions changed slowly over the years. Despite believing my life would be happier and more interesting as a thin person, I also participated in life: two college degrees, a career, marriage, and years of martial arts training. Ultimately it was my participation in life that convinced me my life was already interesting. I didn't need to mold myself into something I wasn't. My happiness was my responsibility. My big body was doing more than many thin-obsessed bodies. This body has been parachuting, white water rafting, and sea kayaking.

I realized weight loss may change one's body, but it doesn't change one's personality, mind, or soul. "The thin person within is not different than the fatter person without," writes Roberta Pollack Seid in *Never Too Thin: Why Women Are at War With Their Bodies*. Seid also observes that when the only purpose of rigid dietary and behavior codes is to change the physical self, "Such actions are not part of a larger system of morals. They don't place value on giving to others. They have no vision of a higher good or of a better future that their rituals might help create."

I have a vision of a future where diversity in all things, including body size, is accepted and even celebrated, and where women (and men) can be comfortable in the bodies they have.

[1] National Institues of Health, "Methods for Voluntary Weight Loss and Control: Technology Assessment Conference Statement," *Nutrition Today*, July-August 1992, p. 27 (7).

[2] Watts, Nelson B., Robert G. Spanheimer, Mario DiGirolamo, Suzanne S.P. Gebhard, Victoria C. Musey, Y. Khalid Siddiq, and Lawrence S. Phillips, "Prediction of Glucose Response to Weight Loss in Patients with Non-Insulin-Dependent Diabetes Mellitus," *Archives of Internal Medicine*, April 1990, p. 803 (4).

[3] Haynes, R.B., "Is Weight Loss an Effective Treatment for Hypertension? The Evidence Against," *Canadian Journal of Physiology and Pharmacology*, Vol. 64, 1986, p. 825 (6).

[4] Polivy, Janet, and C. Peter Herman, "Diagnosis and Treatment of Normal Eating," *Journal of Consulting and Clinical Psychology*, Vol. 55, October 1987, p. 635 (9).

[5] Polivy, Janet, and C. Peter Herman, "Undieting: A Program to Help People Stop Dieting," *International Journal of Eating Disorders*, April 1992, p. 261 (8).

Rosemary E. Knox

Down and Back

Rosemary E. Knox

"Lard butt!"

I heard the words as I was unloading my recyclables at the depot. Looking around, it took me a moment to realize that the words shouted from the passing car were directed at me. I don't think of myself as "fat." Sure, I see a barrel-shaped body in the mirror and I buy my clothes in the sections of stores euphemistically called "woman's world" or some similar title. Why are only large females considered "women" by clothing manufacturers?

"Doesn't it bother you to be so big?" a woman asks me. I stare at her in shock. How rude! Her tone seemed to suggest I should be ashamed of my size. An advice columnist would counsel me to ignore the comment or snap out some phrase politely pointing out her rudeness. I gave the woman an answer. "I've been thin," I said. "The stress wasn't worth it."

Dieting has always thrown me into a state of severe depression. The constant fight to stay away from the foods I love turns me into a neurotic mess. I once succeeded in getting down to a weight society finds acceptable, but it didn't last.

"Nothing tastes as good as thin feels." The hand-lettered placard sat at the front of the room during most of the weight-loss meetings my fiancé and I attended. We recited the saying like a mantra to ourselves over the next few months as we strove to take off our excess poundage. I'd talked my fiancé into dieting with me, depressed by my lack of willpower in the past. We had motivation and a goal, to be thin for our upcoming wedding. We watched every calorie, kept detailed logs of what we ate, and anxiously confronted the scale each week.

I lost over fifty pounds by my wedding day. Thin and happy, I felt like a princess in the size-twelve wedding dress I'd rented. My husband had also reached his goal and looked too handsome for words as we took our vows. Everyone told us we were a beautiful couple.

The first glow from compliments was a delight, but the day-to-day reality of weight maintenance soon became stressful. The familiar plump form I'd known all my life had been replaced by an alien boniness. When I sat in the bathtub, my body's new sharp angles made me squirm to find a comfortable position. I felt so *tiny*. At 5'1", I've never been tall, but now I felt smaller than ever.

The dietary restrictions I was forced to follow began to chafe. I realized keeping the weight off meant I would be forced to be obsessed about every bit of food I ate for the rest of my life. I began to rebel. What was I doing this for? My husband had fallen in love with the fat woman; he didn't care what I weighed. Now that the wedding was over, my motivation fled. I sought new inspiration as the pounds began coming back. The only reason to do this was for *me*, I realized, and I didn't care.

I fell off the wagon and soon was even heavier than before my diet. The guilt was horrible. My husband and I had been written up in the local weight-loss group newsletter when we'd reached our goal. We'd been "good examples" to the other poor souls struggling to lose the unacceptable weight.

The thing was, I didn't feel fat. I felt like me. The thin person had been the impostor.

An acquaintance from the diet group came into work one day, long after I'd gained back all the weight. By then, I'd begun finding peace with my size and was no longer apologetic. She said she'd noticed that I seemed "nervous" when my weight was down, but that I no longer seemed as tense. I realized it was true. I was happier since I quit trying to diet. After numerous attempts to lose the weight again and the dark depression when I failed, I realized I was only dieting because I felt I should. I didn't mind the extra bulk. People are just going to have to accept me as I am, I thought, and if they don't, that's not my problem.

I don't want to become defensive, or wear my weight like a badge of honor. Being heavy is just a part of who I am.

I started buying comfortable clothes, rather than something tight in hopes that I'd soon be taking off a few pounds. The comic strip *Cathy* has become annoying and I often mutter "grow up" as she bemoans the weight she's unable to lose. I quit dieting, ate what I wanted, and found I actually ate less overall. Junk food loses much of its appeal when it isn't "forbidden."

My husband has also gained back his weight, but men are judged by different standards. They are allowed to get old and fat, lose their hair or go gray. Women are supposed to be forever young and beautiful and thin. Ads abound for beauty creams promising to turn back the clock or put our looks in some kind of suspended animation. The ads were once aimed at women over thirty; now they're aimed at teenagers.

Our society gives fat women the message they are "sick" and need help. Weight-loss products and businesses promise to "cure" us of our "affliction." Women starve themselves trying to live up to the ideal in the fashion magazines. Others despair because they can't lose their weight and resign themselves to a life of loneliness and rejection.

Years of searching for approval from the male population added to my own poor self-image. In school, fat girls are sometimes ostracized and ridiculed. Large women are not often asked to dance in bars or singled out for attention at social gatherings. It takes a special type of person to look beneath the surface. That was part of what I craved. I wanted someone who would love *me*, no matter what I looked like. I found that person, or rather, he found me. Through his love, I learned to love myself. My size is irrelevant. I'm the same person now that I was when I weighed 125 pounds. Only now, at 200 pounds, I feel whole. Food is not the "enemy" to be fought. I finally learned to be happy with myself, regardless of my weight.

I've read that girls as young as ten are dieting. I am sad when I think about all the young women who grow up demeaning themselves for being "fat." I was "fat" once. Fat is a state of mind. Self-acceptance can come at any weight. I now hold my head high when I walk, no longer basing my self-worth on my size. A size-eight body does not ensure happiness; happiness comes from within.

Jody Savage

A Family Bouquet

Jody J. Savage

It was the winter of 1975, and I was 22 years old. I had grown up in San Diego and gone to college in Claremont, California. This winter was my first in New York, and I was concerned because my fingers turned white when I went outside. When I left our apartment to go to my appointment with an internist, my boyfriend Dave said, "Ask him if he thinks you should go on a diet."

My white fingers were the result of a harmless syndrome I'd had all my life but never knew about because of my warm-weather upbringing. That question settled, I asked the doctor if I should go on a diet.

"No," he said, "I don't think you need to gain weight." I am 5'6". I weighed 116 pounds that day.

Nine years passed. Dave and I married, finished our graduate degrees (his in law and mine in business), had twin sons, and moved back to California. I put on weight with my twin pregnancy. I put on more with the birth of our daughter. Thin or fat, I was always too fat for my husband.

When our son Jon was born with cerebral palsy, I began the continuing rounds that are part of the job description of the mom of a disabled child—to physical therapists, physicians, equipment providers, and special educators. Later I helped establish the Disabled Children's Computer Group, a technology center for disabled children that became the model for centers like it nationwide. I became the lead plaintiff in a lawsuit that forced my son's school district to make its facilities accessible to wheelchair users. I also began a support group for mothers of twins with disabilities. One of our topics was how to meet the needs of our non-disabled children, like my son Alan who spent so much of his early years as a bystander at his twin's appointments.

Into the midst of this activity was born Diana, a big baby with pink skin and a booming cry. She was born with a subluxed knee, a rare condition in which the knee bends in the wrong direction. During our weekly visits to Stanford Children's Hospital, I helped design a knee brace that corrected her condition without surgery.

When Diana's condition was corrected at seven months, I was in a quandary. On the one hand, acquaintances at Stanford continually told me what a good job I was doing with a challenging mix of circumstances. People I barely knew asked me about my medical background and expressed surprise that I had none. On the other hand, the self I saw in the mirror of my marriage was very different. "You look dumpy." "When are you going to lose weight?" "Why isn't my desk dusted?" "Why wasn't dinner ready when I got home?" These refrains came from my husband. I came to the point where I had to choose which self to accept as reality. I chose to divorce my husband and pursue a second graduate degree, this time in biology. It was 1985. I was 32.

By the time Diana was two years old, her father had begun to tell me she was too fat. He wanted her to be weighed frequently and put on a diet. I knew very little about children and body size, but I knew how indefatigable David could be about fat. My first impulse was to downplay the situation. We engaged in a tug-of-war for several years in which I had the upper hand simply because the children were primarily in my care. But I knew Diana received negative messages about herself at her father's house. I knew how strong those negative messages could be. Diana, being a child, could not choose to walk away as I had. And she had begun to complain about going hungry at her father's house. The result, naturally, was that she became insecure about food and ate a great deal with me.

By 1991 we were in Family Court. I was finishing my Master's degree and returning to full-time employment. We needed to renegotiate our custody arrangements accordingly. And David was seeking a court order to force me to put Diana on a diet. I had decided we needed co-parent counseling and asked the court to order it.

During our rounds of mediation, I read a lot about body size and dieting. At the urging of my lover, Katrinca, I subscribed to *Radiance* magazine. I read Paul Ernsberger's monograph, *Rethinking Obesity*, and the classic *Dieter's Dilemma*. I found books specifically about children: *Are You Too Fat, Ginny?* and that wonderful book with the unfortunate title, *How to Get Your Kid to Eat . . . But Not Too Much* by Ellyn Satter. I joined the National Association to Advance Fat Acceptance (NAAFA). I talked to people in the size-acceptance movement, looking for fat-positive psychologists and nutritionists in our area.

I learned that the model we have lived with for so long, the medical model of obesity, is predicated on a chain of assumptions, each of which is being undermined by current research. Fat people are fat because they eat too much? No, the nutritionists tell us, fat people and thin people on average eat about the same. Fat causes many diseases? No, large body size is associated with a few medical conditions and protects the body from some other medical conditions. Small body size is associated with other medical conditions. Dieting, on the other hand, clearly causes disease. A fat person who diets becomes a thin person? No, a fat person who diets becomes a starving person, with unnaturally small adipose cells. Fat people have shorter life spans? No, moderate obesity is associated with an increased life span.

Our culture promotes an intellectually bankrupt concept of obesity, a concept that our children stand to inherit unless we change it.

One program I investigated was the Shapedown program at University of California - San Francisco. *Radiance* had written about Shapedown because it focused on self-esteem and promoted healthy habits, as opposed to a "diet." The mediator recommended both co-parent counseling and a weight program. We began Shapedown.

Shapedown included much valuable information about nutrition and exercise. Yet the program contained the internal contradictions of a world view in collapse. The program stressed the importance of honesty, but did not contain one word about the health benefits of fat. We discussed the dangers of weightism, yet unhealthy habits were labeled "Fat Habits." We discussed the fact that fat people and thin people eat about the same amount, yet there was continuing discussion of limiting how much our fat children ate. The stated focus was on healthy habits, yet the children were weighed each week. We were told to encourage our children's enjoyment of exercise, yet we were also encouraged to use exercise as a punishment for our children.

"The bottom line for these people," a local author told me, "is that thin is better than fat."

A prominent Bay Area nutritionist was quoted in *Radiance* as saying that any weight management program that does not have weight loss as a goal will have a marketing problem.

As a biologist, I smelled bad science. As a business school graduate, I smelled money. For money, not health, is the heart of this issue. And as a former English major, I smelled a book. I began talking with a New York publisher about writing *To Sell a Pound of Flesh*.

Diana emerged from the Shapedown experience with at least one salient insight. She asked the program leader point-blank one day which was more important: weight loss or healthy habits?

"Healthy habits," Dr. Johnston answered. Thank the Goddess for that answer. At the conclusion of the Shapedown program, we were tested for signs of health problems. We had all been eating well and exercising regularly. Diana was told she needed to be careful, because her blood pressure was a little high—just like her father's.

This last summer, Katrinca and I celebrated our commitment ceremony in the presence of the children and our community of friends and family. Our minister talked about our family as a bouquet of different flowers, each unique and complete, yet complementing each other:

Jon, the first wheelchair user at his middle school, who spoke so eloquently at the press conference announcing the success of our accessibility lawsuit.

Alan, intelligent and caring, already a fine writer, who carries with him the history of his brother's disability and his parents' divorce.

Diana, beautiful and strong, who will need to pick and choose her own way through our culture's obstacle course for women, especially larger women.

Katrinca, Director of Religious Education at our church, concerned stepparent, future minister, who loves me at any size and helped me learn what a true life partnership is.

And me, Jody, mother, fat woman. For me, motherhood is an iterative process: I learn to help my children, then myself. Had Diana been born a little slip of a child, I might have taken much longer to learn what I now know about fat in our society. I might have taken much longer to accept myself as a fat woman. I thank Diana and all the flowers in our family bouquet.

The Still, Small Voice

Sara Greer

"You have no right to be healthy!"

I was seventeen, getting my college-entrance physical. At a little under 5'11", I weighed 245 pounds. The doctor fumed over my test results: heart normal, lungs normal, blood sugar normal, blood pressure lower than normal. He turned to me. "You're as strong as an ox! You're *fat*—you should be in terrible shape." He brightened, saved by an afterthought. "Just you wait, young lady. Some day it's going to catch up to you. I bet you'll have high blood pressure by the time you're thirty if you don't get rid of that lard."

My mother (also fat), whose doctor he was, sat quietly through the lecture. Afterward, on the way to the car where my father waited, she said, "He's right, you know. You should lose some weight." Hypertensive and diabetic, she was a strong believer in what-the-doctor-says, and had been a yo-yo dieter for over thirty years. She had said the same thing to me nine years before, when my pediatrician had scolded me for being five pounds overweight. "That's a lot for an eight-year-old," he told me. "If you're not careful, you'll be fat when you grow up."

Back then, I'd listened to my mother and the doctor, and went on my first diet. At seventeen, I wasn't about to go on another diet to please an officious jerk. That rejection was the first step on my journey toward accepting my size and a catalyst of the seeds of change, provoking the first faint whispers of the still, small voice of rebellion that would later rise to a shout.

That first diet, at age eight, had begun the process of smothering that voice. From the first, my deep internal reaction had been one of rebellion, a refusal to believe that I could have something so dreadfully wrong with me when I felt just fine. I spent a lot of time looking at myself in the bathroom mirror, seeking comprehension of a flaw seen by others but unperceivable to me—wondering what unwitting sin I was guilty of, while deep inside me a voice cried, "What's *wrong* with me? What did I *do*?" But I lacked the introspection or insight to solve the riddle, and I had been programmed all my life by a combination of Catholic guilt and my mother's struggles with her size. So I gradually learned to hate my apparently defective flesh, stifled the protests, and made myself deaf to that inner voice. Nine years later I heard, once again, the first faint murmur: "What's *wrong* with me?"

I didn't particularly analyze my reaction at seventeen, either; I simply felt and enjoyed the rebellion, the sense of having scored off an adversary. The journey continued as quietly as it began. In college, the voice of protest came and went, with varying degrees of loudness. I gained forty pounds the first year. With no Mom around to control the overeating end of the diet and gorge cycle, and with the underlying sense of rebellion to fuel it, I alternately starved and stuffed, ate almost nothing or indulged in big meals and lots of snacks. I told myself the problem was the dorm food, kept wedging myself into the same size jeans (the largest size the store carried—men's, of course), and kept dieting off and on.

My first boyfriend exploited my size. He confided to me once that he "loved fat girls," only later adding "because they're desperate." At that, the quiet voice set up such a clamor that not even the extra forty pounds could still it, and I dumped him. Later dates "tactfully" ignored my fat, pretending it didn't exist: more stimulus for the voice. Why should I only exist from the neck up? The diets were gradually growing farther apart, shorter in duration, less drastic.

In 1982, I met my future husband. First as a friend and later as a lover, he often expressed pleasure in my looks. It was a revelation to find that some men did love fat women, not exploiting their "desperation" but admiring their beauty. He gave me a lot of support for my appearance, replacing the denigration of others with help in finding clothes that fit and flattered and with frequent assurances of how beautiful I was—not merely in his eyes, but absolutely. He coaxed me out of those too-tight jeans and into the roomy comfort of parachute pants, whereupon half my back problems (and several other minor health problems) disappeared.

In my growing sense of freedom and self-confidence, I decided to find out how much I weighed. I hadn't been on a scale in three years, my diets having been gauged by the fit of my clothing—a system that no longer worked in my new, looser clothing. I knew, of course, which department store ladies' lounge had the only scale in town that was accurate at higher weights. The scale was a huge, old-fashioned thing that had fascinated me as a child. It was left over from a time when women were encouraged to have substance, if only physically, and it went up to 450 pounds. I waited until the room was empty and stepped on.

It was a severe setback. I didn't yet know about the yo-yo dieting boobytrap, which had apparently affected me with more severity as I matured, and I was unaware of how much I had gained back after my last diet. So I nearly fainted when the scales rattled and the pointer swung around to 306 pounds.

I rationalized, of course. I estimated the weight of my clothes, kicked off my shoes, and tried again—but I had to face the fact that nude or clothed, shod or not, I weighed somewhere around 300 pounds. Forgetting my height and the weight of my bones (so heavy that as a child I would sink in water unless I had lungs full of air), I felt like a grotesque blimp of fat. I crept home and began another diet, my last, one more futile attempt to fight what I was and ignore that inner voice.

My husband was dubious, having little faith in diets, but he was supportive of my right to choose what to do with my body. For most of a summer, I ate cantaloupe until I thought I'd turn orange, chewed celery until I expected my footsteps to crunch. I lost twenty-four pounds with seductive and amazing rapidity—in six weeks. I thought that at last I would make it to 180 pounds, a goal I had long since abjured.

But the weight began to creep back even though I was scrupulously following the diet—one pound, two, three, five. I couldn't stop it. I agonized for two weeks. Then something within me finally snapped, and I walked out of the dilemma. I could just quit dieting. So I quit; I ate normally and watched the pounds return, thirty-six in all. There my weight stabilized, and there I let it rest. At age twenty-four, after sixteen years on the diet merry-go-round, I stepped off.

Stepping off was easy. Staying off was another matter. I had mostly negative feedback, including some from my own internal programming. The reactions of most friends and family members generally fell into the "3-D" range: disdain ("Are you crazy?"), dismissal ("Oh? Well, I'm sure you'll be dieting again soon."), or disbelief ("What did you say? You're kidding, right?"). One friend in nursing school had arrived at much the same conclusion and essentially agreed with my choice. Another friend, fat, embraced size-acceptance wholeheartedly only to reject it with equal vehemence later. My husband gave me unqualified support, helping me to defuse the programming that battered me from within and to set aside the put-downs and rejections that came from without—especially the subtle abusiveness of the few who tried "tactfully" to talk me out of it "for my own good."

One of the worst struggles I faced, and probably the most critical, was learning how to eat normally. Sixteen years of dieting and overeating had destroyed the natural processes and mechanisms of hunger, satiety, and choosing what and how much to eat and drink. All my behavior patterns were correspondingly distorted, and I faced the task of building new ones.

I began by trying to listen to my body, eating when I thought I was hungry, stopping when I thought I was full, eating what I thought my body wanted. I found that my body "wanted" things that made me feel ill or things that I disliked. I'll never forget the day when I discovered that I actually hated the Cheetos I'd been eating by the bag for years. I bought a large bag, opened it, and ate one Cheeto when I realized that it tasted horrible. Borrowing an idea from a book I'd read, I stapled the bag shut, jumped up and down on it, and carefully poured the greasy orange mess into the garbage. Freedom! I stopped eating these foods and gradually stopped craving them. I also rediscovered the joys of healthy, "low-cal" foods, especially vegetables, that I had once loved but had grown sick of. Sometimes I ate entire meals of them—a huge bowl of homemade cole-slaw—savoring every crunchy, delicious bite. I no longer *had* to eat them, so I began to *want* to eat them.

I made many mistakes, often eating too much or too little, sometimes eating the wrong foods. Even eight years later, this still happens now and again. Such large-scale damage takes time to heal completely. I make progress day by day.

The other great struggle was, and is, dealing with the criticism, put-downs, rejection, and abuse from without or within. Years of repeated diets and repeated failures had instilled a deep sense of incompetence and unworthiness in me, producing internal messages of self-hate ranging from the bludgeons of "You deserve to fail" and "You're a worthless fool" to the subtler knife-in-the-ribs of "Of course it didn't work out." And there were self-created failures, many of them, stupid mistakes, careless lack of attention, verbal blunders.

Slowly and with painful care, I held written dialogues with myself, drawing lines of truce, finding the roots of negative messages, disarming their weapons, and destroying them. Equally slowly and carefully, I planted the seeds of healing, beginning to instill positive messages, looking for my skills and good points and fostering their growth, pampering myself some-times. In both efforts, my husband offered support and guidance. He realized that because I had been systematically taught to place others' valuation of me above my own, I would need positive messages from outside until I could learn to create and listen to my own. He made mistakes, as I did (and still do), but he worked carefully and hard to support me in a way that would build my strength and increase my ability to support myself. It is an ongoing process, and healing is well underway.

The abuse from without is more difficult to limit, so instead I have worked on shaping my response to it. I had some spectacular failures, arising pri-marily out of the huge reserve of anger and pain that I had not yet drained. Once, a total stranger approached me at a bus stop—a woman who was agonizingly thin, famine thin. She said, "You're really gross! I can't believe how fat you are. I'd kill myself if I looked like you. You're disgusting!" I won't repeat what I said to her; even seven years later, I'm ashamed of it. It was quick, cruel, and effective, and it taught me a valuable lesson: not to respond in anger. The face I turn on insulting people now is one of puzzle-ment, coupled with a comment like, "I beg your pardon?" On days when my control is less good, I tend to say, "Why do you think I value your opinion?"

I learned other lessons: how to walk tall and straight, not trying to hide my height or my belly; how to ignore the insults leveled at me by teenagers, especially boys, who are delighted by any response except no response; how to report derisive sexual harassment (my boss was astonishingly supportive, although he had originally told my supervisor not to hire me because of my size); and how to wear buttons with size-positive messages.

I dealt with my fear of strangers and my fear of being noticed by getting a public contact job, which taught me that I love to work with people. I still feel sometimes that I would rather hide than deal with a stranger, and I still hate parties unless I know several people present. I do have days when I want to meet some fat-basher's remarks with a curled lip and a resounding "F--k you!" But I have learned the most important lesson, to love and accept myself. If I still forget it now and then, all the same my journey is well underway and the still, small voice that began the journey is louder and stronger. At thirty-two, I am happier about my body, and healthier, than I have ever been, and the scenery along the road is looking better every day.

PS. Hey doc, you lose your bet!

Sondra Solovay
(second from right)

Now You See Me, Now You . . .

Sondra Solovay

*"I'll wait until December. That's five and a half months.
If I'm not really thin by Christmas then I can kill myself."*
—*a ten-year-old girl*

*"I'm not going to college like this.
If I don't lose enough to look good, I'm not going."*
—*same girl, eight years later*

This story could easily be another of lost potential, but it is not. I managed to go to college despite the fact that I had not lost the weight. Four years later, a different person graduated.

Since high school I had been outspoken on issues of feminism. I arrived at college with experience in theatre and public speaking, and by the end of my second month I had given a speech to hundreds of students about the importance of keeping abortion legal and accessible. Abortion rights interested me because I could see how systematically and effectively women were being barred from positions of power. My outrage at the prospect of making abortion illegal and immoral grew from my belief in a woman's right to autonomy over her body. Women are taught that using their bodies to serve themselves, to please themselves, is selfish. For anti-choice people in the abortion debate, a woman's body belongs first to the fetus. To place a woman out of control of her own body was insane, of this I was confident.

Although I was far from realizing it at the time, these arguments mirror those used by the diet industry. The diet culture attempts to control women's bodies by dictating standards of health and morality. That culture often claims a woman's body belongs first to men's desires, which the diet industry constructs. Even if a woman is not aware that the marriage of slenderness and morality started in the nineteenth century, almost every dieter is familiar with the internalized ties between thinness and ethics: I was *bad* at the wedding, but I'll be *good* next week.

Realizing I was well-known for giving speeches on political issues, a student approached me and asked me to give a speech for Body Image Awareness Week. She told me two other people, an anorexic and a bulimic, would be speaking. With artificial calm I declined, quickly heading for a bathroom. If the world had suddenly come to a grinding halt, I could not have been more taken aback. I focused on breathing. Of course I knew there were few fat people at Brown University. I knew one other woman in passing, but rarely did I see anyone who would have been directed by the weight charts to lose more than twenty pounds.

Why me? Why did she have to ask me? What right did she have to come up to me? To ask me to speak about that? Was I supposed to talk about my implied eating disorder? I was furious, and I was scared. The I'm-just-like-everyone-else game had been going so well, I had forgotten I looked different. I had forgotten I was being judged every second I was looked at. Suddenly I felt completely alone. I was. No one in school was defending the right to be large. Bulimics were not being told "It's okay to be fat." They were being told "Don't worry, you are not fat." I had never heard of the National Association to Advance Fat Acceptance (NAAFA). All I knew was that I had a hard time buying clothes I liked, and large models wore size twelve. I felt like crying all the time. In classes I replayed the student's question over and over in my head. Finally, I realized that my reaction was crazy. If one person's comment could put me out of commission for days, there was a problem that needed my attention.

I decided to attempt to analyze calmly even the most painful weight-related experiences as they came up. I also resolved to rethink my definition of beauty and the ideal body, opening my mind to different appearances. At the time I did not realize how revolutionary these two steps were, nor was I prepared for the magnitude of the project.

Immediately my classes were affected. As a first-year student I pursued drama classes, where I was systematically handed mother roles. This typecasting happened because few mother roles involve sexuality, and fat women are seen as undesirable and asexual. Never would I be given the role of Juliet, and I had played one too many Lady Capulets. What had been discouragement turned to rebellion. Sensing an unwinnable fight, I decided not to deal with those people, and left mainstage theatre for an innovative, collaborative group, Awareness Theatre, which casts "without regard for anything, at all."

Size harassment and weight discrimination are not passive institutions that one can choose to leave behind. In the dining hall, a conversation at the next table, a student titters, "So he asks me 'Which one is she?' and, like, I don't know what to say." Nods, smiles, and giggles of encouragement abound. "So I'm like 'She's the fat girl.' I feel bad calling her that but, I mean, she is, ya know? (giggle) I mean, how else should I describe her?

Overweight? Big? Boat-like? It's not like she heard me anyway. So I just said, 'She's the fat girl.' What else could I say?"

Why didn't you say, "She's the beautiful one," or "She's the one in the red shirt," or "She's the third from the left," or "The one with long hair," I wanted to ask. "Why is the only thing you notice about women their body size?" I should have demanded. But my pledge was to analyze. My analysis told me these people were simply not looking for an acceptable way to identify a woman, and they were not trying to de-stigmatize the word "fat." They were bonding by bringing up a fat girl they all knew and making her an outsider. I walked by their table. They stopped talking until I passed, then continued, "Oh my God, I feel so bad. (giggle, giggle) Did she hear us? (giggle)"

Shortly afterward I was sitting outside and two women rode by on bicycles. One shouted, "Jenny Craig's open on Saturdays!" (The woman is lucky she rode away fast.) Still, despite my analytical powers, she got to me. Did she really think I wasn't obsessed with my eating? That I did not know what I looked like? I went to sleep angry at her. I woke up and made two vows: (1) I was not going to waste any more time chastising myself over food, no more dieting, and (2) I was going to talk back however I could.

These promises changed my life. Deciding not to diet felt like being zapped from a subway at rush hour to an open field. Everyone who has dieted knows what it's like not to be dieting, but few know what it's like not to diet at all. It's empty. It takes getting used to. Suddenly there was no need to count calories each day. No voice was saying, "Sondra, you shouldn't have eaten that." I had to make up new things to think about as I drifted off to sleep. I could no longer postpone activities until I was thin, because I was not going to lose weight.

This one decision, firmly adhered to, removed me from the insanity of the weight-loss cult. From the outside, it sure looks crazy in there. I realized that character was not determined by dieting and body size, and beauty was an image that repeatedly changes. Further, those women and men who spent hours and hours and hundreds of dollars to keep their bodies thin were just as brainwashed as I had been. Those who seemed holy in their righteousness became immature name callers. Those who professed to "help" demonstrated their ignorance.

The second pledge manifested itself concretely. While I used to wonder if I should respond to rude and uneducated comments, and rarely got around to considering how to do it, now I had the responsibility to do something. Because I do not respond well on the spot, I had to find another way to speak out against size discrimination. My answer, performance.

Awareness Theatre creates its own performances and scripts collaboratively to increase awareness of various social issues. We agreed to do a piece on body image. After trying to discuss the issues, an extraordinarily difficult task, we finally talked about our personal histories. Every woman in the group had experienced or witnessed abnormal eating behaviors, vomiting being the norm. For the first time I related my three hours exercise and 300-calories-every-other-day diet from junior high school. In the piece we scripted, I did not stand up and say, "Fat is beautiful and so am I." But I was in the piece, and it marked the beginning of my fight to change attitudes about fat women.

My friends saw a shift in my television-watching patterns. In the past when we watched the dormitory television and a weight-loss advertisement came on, I would either try to distract the group by talking loudly, or leave the room. The "new me" made everyone quiet down so I could hear the voice-over. I took notes and wrote papers about the diet advertisements for English classes. I studied the rhetorical strategies used to convince people that losing weight was required for happiness. Some weight-loss advertisements appeal to the Judeo-Christian ethic of Guilt and Redemption by labeling nourishment "sinful" while pushing their own pre-packaged frozen "goodness" or through tearful confessions by distraught, guilt-ridden women who, having admitted their weakness, are saved not with diets but with a "new lifestyle." Other advertisements use the device of Forced Choice. Forced Choice presents two options, as if they were the only options. Usually fat is aligned with laziness, social isolation, exhaustion, depression, ugliness, old age, incapacitation, sickness, shame, lack of control, dissatisfaction, sexlessness, and even evil. Thinness is paired with all the "good" things: energy, popularity, activity, happiness, beauty, youth, ability, health, pride, control, satisfaction, sexual attractiveness, and joy. Omitted is the continuum of body sizes and the possibility of being fat and sexy or thin and exhausted.

Around the time Oprah Winfrey lost weight, a downtown theatre put together a program to protest the impending censorship of art. The lack of fat women in the media stood out to me as a glaring omission, exemplifying the constant, present censorship of women of substance in the public eye. In my piece a woman of size addresses the audience, handing out magazine pictures:

"Censorship! Censorship! We will have it! We won't have it! We do. You do. You censor, you do. See? You missed it. Watch them. Look at what we don't see in magazines, and on TV, except as butts, of jokes. And such Big-butt jokes. I'm saying it as clearly as I can: Look at what's not there already. You. Yes, you. Look. You look. Look, you frighten me. The absences you don't see. The beauty you don't see. What don't you see? What don't you see? Look at your stomach. What don't you see? Look at your magazines. What don't you see? Twenty-eight percent. Twenty-eight percent of Americans. And we are big. So big we can't be seen."

I was not silenced in college. Because my politics were liberal, my art and performances bold, and my tastes non-traditional, I avoided the full force of one the toughest problems for a young fat woman, perhaps for any fat woman: intimacy. Dating is much harder for a fat woman because, no matter how special or smart or charming she is, her lover has to be strong enough to realize she is beautiful and sexy and be confident enough to defend that view to the world. Since most fat women have a hard time feeling good about themselves and would choose to be thin if offered a magic pill, it is understandable that a lover would have similar feelings.

I was lucky. I have never been the kind of person who needed a partner to feel complete. My friends satisfied me, and my weight never came up as an issue with them. Because I was so involved with the creative community, I found more open-minded lovers than the average person. I was visible and unique; these characteristics made me attractive. Because I had done research and knew that the beauty ideal was completely arbitrary, I was confident and comfortable in bed. Still, there were problems. I have found people attracted to my size, not to me. I have also had people interested in me *despite* my size. We are more than these isolated pieces. We deserve to be appreciated both physically and mentally. We deserve to be with people who find us beautiful.

Awareness Theatre did a second piece on body image, "Barbie and Ken Don't Live Here Anymore." In it I delivered this speech for hundreds of students:

"I'm going to begin my talk by asking you to close your eyes. Now, clear your mind. Relax. Okay. Take a minute, and picture a beautiful woman. Get her set in your mind. Move in closer to your image. Notice her body, her stance. Move closer. Look at her face. Remember her eyes, her hair, her skin. Keep this image in your mind and open your eyes.

"I am going to ask a few questions. Did the woman you pictured have a skin color different from your own? Was she over thirty years of age? Did you imagine someone who was not thin? Was your picture of a woman who had a disability? A mastectomy? Were all her features perfectly symmetrical? Was she the kind of woman who could appear on the cover of a fashion magazine?

"It seems strange that though we could not agree on what constitutes a beautiful sweater, we can come up with a definition of beauty for women that is almost identical. Why do we have a similar definition of beauty? First of all, we have to realize that beauty is socially constructed. Different cultures have different ideals. Even in the same culture, different time periods produce different ideas of beauty. Just short periods of time can demonstrate significant differences in images of beauty. Think of the difference between Marilyn Monroe, Twiggy, and Cindy Crawford.

"A major problem with the beauty ideal today is that it no longer fluctuates naturally. Our culture is now heavily influenced, if not controlled, by big industries like the fashion industry, the cosmetics industry, and the diet industry. These businesses have fortunes at stake. The cosmetics industry is twenty billion dollars a year, the diet industry is a thirty-three-billion-dollar-a-year business. That money is made by showing one definition of beauty, and claiming that this product or that product makes it available to us.

"But so what? Why should we worry about where our ideas of beauty come from and what they are? The answer is twofold. Number one is simple: Our rigid definition hurts people, especially women. The diet industry is certainly not going to tell us that only two to five percent of people lose weight permanently. They make their thirty-three billion by hiding the fact that ninety-eight percent of people will fail. Since they don't know that they cannot succeed, dieters feel guilty and worthless as they put on more weight than they lost. Anorexia and bulimia are affecting young women in record numbers. And if only there was a way to evaluate the hours of time and energy spent worrying and thinking about weight loss . . . Further, yo-yo dieting actually increases the risk of serious disease in all patients from thirty to one hundred percent.

"The second reason we need to re-examine our definition of beauty is philosophical. What we think of as our own taste may not be. We have been handed an image from such a young age and have seen only that picture for so long, that many of us have been manipulated into adopting it as Beauty. No questions asked. A few years ago I began to examine the image of beauty I had in my head. I realized suddenly that it was not mine. None of my creativity, my tastes, my desires, none of me had gone into my definition of beauty. I had adopted, without thinking, somebody else's standards.

"So I leave you with a challenge. Look at the Cover Girl "Redefining Beautiful" campaign. Note that there is no redefinition of beauty at all. Examine your definition of beauty, see if it is yours. If not, try to redefine beauty. See if you can be more successful, more creative, more respectful than Cover Girl Cosmetics."

When I was in grade school, a story similar to the following, told by a young girl, appeared in the Weight Watchers Camp brochure. The story convinced me to go to the camp:

"On the last day all your camp friends are sitting around waiting for their families to drive up. All the parents are so surprised to see how thin their fat daughters have gotten in just two months. And then I saw my family. They just looked at me like they couldn't believe it. And I was so proud. I could tell they were so proud of me. My brother ran up to me and grabbed me in his arms. He picked me up and spun me around and around and around. He said, 'I never thought I'd be able to pick you up,' as he smiled from ear to ear. I smiled too because the thin girl inside of me finally got to come out."

I have changed these past four years. I no longer want to be proud of myself for being less substantial. I no longer consider it a compliment to be told I look good because there's less of me to look at. I no longer accept the idea that the strength of one's character is determined by one's willpower, and I certainly do not agree that the daily measuring of one level scoop of powdered drink and the consuming of premeasured frozen dinners reflect an individual's control over food.

I recognize those people who refuse to question prevailing standards of beauty as cultural dupes. But most of all, I want to state loudly to this story-brother and all the real brothers, boyfriends, husbands, and men: There is no thin girl inside me waiting, wanting to be picked up and swung around. Nowhere in the depth of my being do I harbor the desire to be lifted off the ground, light and maneuverable, to be tossed about like a doll. I am not a doll. I am a woman.

Lou Ann Thomas

A Woman of Size

Lou Ann Thomas

I am a large woman, a woman of size, a woman of substance, an Amazon, Earth Mother. These labels I have begun to choose for myself. Fatty, Fatso, and Tubby are labels that others have always given me. At first it was the chants and calls of other children when I began to gain weight in grade school. Later it became the whispered chiding and teasing of high school peers. Then it often came as disapproving looks, sometimes even pity in the eyes of other adults. "It" is the prejudice and lack of understanding and acceptance for large women.

Growing up I had no role models for loving myself as a large woman, for loving myself as a woman, period. There certainly weren't large actresses or models presented in a way that encouraged acceptance and love. Even catalogs for large-size clothes used thin models. The message was that large women aren't even attractive enough to model our own clothes. My parents and friends constantly picked at me, trying to get me to lose weight. Their motivation may have been one of love and concern, but the result was I got a clear message that how I was, how I looked, wasn't good enough, wasn't lovable, wasn't acceptable. I soon took on this attitude about myself and believed it as truth.

I began to believe I was unlovable. I believed that if anyone did love me they loved me for some ulterior motive, some hidden agenda, certainly not because I was lovable and most definitely not because I was attractive or desirable. This attitude is not conducive to fostering long-term, mutually loving, and open relationships. I was convinced that I was to live a very lonely and alone life simply because I was "fat."

My parents said things like, "You would be really attractive *if* you would lose weight." Or "We would be so proud of you if you would lose weight." Even my parents couldn't accept me as I was; how in the world could I ever expect anyone else to accept and love me for me? This task seemed impossible. In a way it was, and still is, impossible—certainly unlikely that anyone would love and accept me as I was until I learned to love and accept myself as I was. Now that is a task, but not an impossible one.

I had experienced over thirty-five years of conditioning telling me that I was unacceptable, but bit by bit, piece by piece, I am learning to rewrite those messages to myself. I wish I could tell you here's how you do it in twelve easy steps or give you ten days to loving and accepting yourself. But I can't, because learning to love and accept myself has been a long, sometimes slow, journey that has taken me through my own prejudices about fat, flesh, and friendship. I had to acknowledge my hangups about weight and body size and how those hangups reflected the age-old teaching of my family and of society that somehow large is less than.

My journey to self-acceptance has taken me through some dark places within myself, places that I didn't know existed before I began this odyssey. I have seen how attached I was to what others saw and believed me to be. I have found the same looks of unacceptance and pity in my own eyes and have had to deal with my prejudices and misconceptions about large women. I have become aware of the stream of negative self-talk that constantly jabbered in my head. I have learned how to begin to change those messages and that self-destructive chatter.

For me this process is ongoing. Everyday I come out a little more as a large woman, woman of substance, Earth Mother. Each day I learn a little more about myself, the dark side of prejudices and conditions as well as the light side of acceptance and love. Once I began this journey, the positive self-attitude gained momentum and now seems to have a life of its own. I am no longer comfortable believing, or even listening to, the negative talk or buying into the way someone else sees me. If someone sees something unacceptable or unlovable when they look at me, that fact says more about those people and their prejudices than it does about me.

Being in my body has always been hard for me. I have lived most of my life in my head, rarely moving down into my body despite years as a high school and college athlete. As I progress in loving and accepting myself, I am making fast friends with my body. I now feel great joy in dancing and walking and moving my body in graceful and strong ways. My body has been an amazing tool that has served me exceptionally well, and I want to learn to take good care of it, to celebrate and protect it, and to move it in ways that are pleasing and beautiful.

I needed time to learn to love flesh, to begin to see my large body as beautiful, as attractive, and as desirable. I used to avoid my reflection in mirrors and windows. Shopping was torture for me and window shopping was agony because I always saw my reflection first, and I hated it. I began to change my feeling that my body wasn't attractive by spending time in front of the mirror admiring my body. It was pure Hell at first. I could hardly stand to look at myself, much less say something positive about my body. I kept at this process because, frankly, I am worth it. Soon my view of my flesh, my round belly, and my full breasts began to change.

Lately I have been enjoying my reflection more and more, maybe because it no longer reflects those old, terribly hurtful messages from others, and is now a more clear reflection of a woman who cares about and loves herself. The other day I glanced in a store window as I walked by and thought, "That's a beautiful woman." I walked a few more feet before it hit me that my thought had been about my own reflection.

Diane L. Lambson
(middle)

It Ain't Over 'Til the Fat Lady Sings

Diana L. Lambson

"It ain't over 'til the fat lady sings, and I'm not singing yet!"

One will yell the strangest things in the heat of the first round of play-offs for the state championship in six-man football, especially when one's son is on the field. Ten years ago I may have said it in a self-deprecating way, but I wouldn't have screamed it at the top of my lungs in a crowd of more than 600 people. It's been a long time coming.

Like most overweight Americans, I have spent most of my life listening to kids call me names like Tub-of-Lard, Fatty, Bertha Big Belly, Two Ton Tessy, etc. I've also listened to well-meaning adults hint gently, and not so gently, that I needed to lose weight. They said I would feel so much better about myself. How did they know how I felt? Did they realize by that very statement they were creating a self-image so poor I still have problems with it? Maybe they did. Maybe they didn't. Whatever the case, I spent years thinking I was not worth looking at, talking or listening to, or being with. Like most others in the same boat, I think I've tried every diet, including the rainbow pill doctors who were so popular in the late 1960s.

I actually did lose seventy pounds as a senior in high school. Even then, when I joined the U.S. Navy after high school graduation, I spent the whole time of my enlistment on the pudgy platoon. I even managed to get down to 145 pounds. (I had weighed 225 pounds, and I'm 5'9" tall.) At 145, on my frame, I had no chest, no behind, and no discernible waist. I resembled a one-by-twelve board on a yard fence, but the board still saw itself as blobby fat, so I nearly became anorexic, eating only one very small meal a day and feeling guilty about that. I got so run-down, I contracted mononucleosis and ended up in the hospital.

That's life! I now know I will never have an hour-glass figure, but I do have redeeming qualities. Besides, I'm forty-five, not nineteen, and I hope I've grown beyond the purely physical. It didn't dawn on me, though, how I had contributed to my poor self-image until I listened to what I said to my daughter as she was growing up.

She also is large, though her weight tends to be closer to the ground. She is only 5'6" tall and instead of carrying her weight above her hips as I do, she carries it on her hips with large thighs and buttocks. She has beautiful, creamy skin and blonde hair, and when she smiles the room lights up. She inherited her father's mischievous grin.

I often repeated to her that she could not depend on others to make her happy. She must find happiness within herself. Her father and I also stressed that what one looks like on the outside has nothing to do with that person's worth as a human being. We're firm believers in the old adage, "Beauty is as beauty does." We often said people who belittle others only do so because they feel so small themselves they need to make someone else even smaller to feel better.

Suddenly, I realized I should practice what I preached. I wasted most of my life feeling inferior because others felt that way about themselves. They solved their problems by acting out against me. They may have behaved in a poor fashion, but I compounded it by believing them.

Now, I know differently. I am a worthy person, even though I do not wear a size six. I am learning to develop my God-given talents and, surprisingly, finding even more. I have learned to be outgoing. That is my nature but a neurotic society taught me well that a large, friendly, outgoing, fairly intelligent, self-assured woman is not welcome. Therefore, I cringed in the corners of rooms at gatherings and when no one approached me it reinforced my belief that was where I belonged.

Since I became a correspondent for a daily newspaper and active at the synod level of my church, I have realized I have something worth saying and listening to. I no longer cringe, I initiate, and people do listen. In fact, they smile at me and sometimes even seek me out in a crowd. And, if they are overwhelmed by my size, that's their problem.

I do have to be careful of my diet. Periodic depression and approaching menopause tend to throw me for a loop, and I often find myself binge eating during stressful times, especially if they occur with ovulation. But once I recognize the behavior, I curb it by keeping busy with one of my many activities or going for a walk. That seems to help, and I get the benefit of fresh air too.

I do have a long way to go yet. I still feel guilty every time I put food in my mouth, even when it's mealtime and maintenance eating. For a long time I listened to and believed the awful myth, "Fat people have no willpower. They must punish themselves by not eating and when they do eat it's because they are uncaring, fat slobs. If they cared they would be thin." Old habits are hard to break.

That's a heavy burden to ask anyone to bear. Unfortunately, we now demand that young women and girls be increasingly thin and so the burden is carried on and our young women die, mentally and physically.

However, I have confidence I will overcome. I also fervently hope society soon wises up. Besides, it ain't over 'til the fat lady sings, and I ain't singing yet!

The Heroine and the Harpy

Fiona Webster

As I look back down the path from where I am now, a happy fat woman, to where I was before, a miserable dieting woman, I'm reminded of a fantasy quest—an adventurous voyage of a doubtful heroine through often-hostile lands. Along the way I encountered various monsters: my family's wishes for me, my classmates' social pressure, expectations from society, clinical depression, and most fearsome of all, my relentless self-criticism. I endured torture in the dungeon of enforced starvation. I was stretched on the rack of excessive exercise. I quailed before wizardly illusions of my body as a grotesque and loathsome creature. Mirrors assailed me, shopping malls challenged me, and the clothes closet in my bedroom was a thicket of dread and guilt. When at last I broke free into open, sunny country, clutching tightly the treasured amulet of self-acceptance, for a while I stumbled about in amazement. How did this happen? Wasn't it my destiny to always be miserable about being fat?

Nearly four years later, four remarkable years during which my weight has remained the same, the first such period in my whole life, I am still staring about in wonder. When I get up in the morning, I look in the mirror and see a beautiful woman gazing back at me. When I open my closet door, I see clothes that are like old friends—clothes I've worn for years now and have confidence in. When I walk out the door into the wide outdoors, I walk without fear of disapproval. The suffering, which had seemed endless, is over.

In the fantasy tales, the heroes and heroines are almost always depicted as young people, as supercharged, idealistic adolescents. To retrace the steps of my personal adventure and find the bend in the trail where the monsters began to lose power and the changes began to appear, I have to go back to when I was first discovering that maybe youth was not, as had been advertised, the best part of life.

I knew the years before thirty were supposed to be a turbulent time, a time of sweeping emotions and deep, existential uncertainties, but I never figured the storms would hurt me in any lasting way. I rued the condition of my figure—always, no matter how thin I was, I thought I was too fat—

but in the area of inner resources, I saw myself as infinitely resilient, infinitely energetic. I thought that my psyche was in its prime and that all my years of education were shaping me into a mental athlete—a well-oiled machine, a machine that always performed correctly.

But the years between twenty and thirty were much harder than I'd expected, so I had to rethink my assumptions. Maybe my psyche wasn't put together as well as I'd thought. Maybe it wasn't a smoothly coordinated system at all, but rather a collection of mismatched parts and leftover pieces. Some of these parts were so poorly put together, they seemed designed to sabotage me at every turn. I discovered that my inner self suffered pain far more often than did my physical self. My inner self always moaned or groaned about something, and gloomy thoughts started clogging the gears.

The worst of these thoughts were the thoughts about my body.

You must understand, my body itself was never really the problem. I was of a moderate size. People didn't jeer at me in the street. I wasn't turned away at the door of life on the grounds of being too fat. No, it was always in the inner world, the world of my thoughts, where the monsters arose.

I recall especially my fear and loathing on the way to getting dressed every morning. Approaching my closet was a trial of courage, and when I opened the door, I saw clothes that didn't fit. They were like demons taunting me, all those clothes that were too small to wear: the soft cotton blouses, the straight skirts, the tailored blazers, the narrow-waisted trousers. I'd had little chance to wear them, so they seemed immortal, always new. "Why do they have to be so lovely?" I used to cry. Why was it always, and only, during my fleeting windows of slenderness that I bought these pretty clothes—these way-too-many, infuriating, expensive doll clothes for a doll I didn't own? What I did have to wear, on any one day, was limited to a painfully meager assembly of less desirable items. It seemed I had an uncanny ability to gain just enough weight that I would have a few unattractive things that fit, and rarely enough weight to justify new purchases. The exact formula, in other words, for misery.

I know I struggled with my clothes, tokens of my failure at the task of physical appearance, because (it's trite, but true) women in our culture are raised to see ourselves as aesthetic objects. I can remember when I was an adolescent, reading *Seventeen* magazine during the sixties—the articles on makeup, on figure flaws, on dos and don'ts of fashion. My friends and I sat around and poured over those glossy, colored pages as if they were infallible blueprints for life. At the time, femininity, as depicted in the magazines, was abandoning its old stance of passive eroticism. The models we saw stared purposefully into the viewer's eyes. The image of the new woman we absorbed was one of an unashamed person, fully in control of her life.

Yet my classmates and I, as growing teenagers, were not so bold. We were scared of our growing body parts. We even used to punish each other for the changes of puberty: We had a cruel game of running up to someone suddenly, punching her on her tender new breasts, then laughing as she tried not to cry out in pain. It seemed to us that everything we thought of as "gross," all the disturbing mysteries of female sexuality, came down to one thing—body fat: body fat in the new breasts and hips, body fat labeled as unwanted, body fat seen as evidence of being out of control.

My response to these pressures was hardly unique. I ate sweets to assuage the fears, I gained weight, I dieted, I lost weight, I gained more weight. Slowly I expanded from a slim pre-teen, to a shapely teen, to a chubby adult. I kept up with the dictatorial fashion magazines, as they marched in their ever-unfolding, ever-new images of the same old story: "The most important thing in a woman's life is a slender physique." But with time, I didn't need to hear the messages from the media anymore. I took the obsession with slenderness inside me, where it acquired a life of its own. A personally-designed, hand-tailored weight critic took up residence in my brain.

Even now, I shudder to think of that fearsome, exasperating, never-silent weight critic. Of all the monsters I encountered during my journey, this one was the worst. In later years, after I'd gotten to know the monster better, I started calling her the Harpy. The mythological harpies are described as fair-haired women with swift wings and fierce tempers. I have blonde hair myself, so when I imagined this critical self who had established herself in a position of judgment within my head, I saw her as fair, thin (of course), and mercilessly competent. The assigned job of the harpies (the word means "the snatchers") is to swoop down on criminals and carry them away for punishment. That's what my harpy did: I was the one being snatched. In some Greek tales, the "criminals" are innocent children being punished for the sins of their parents. Three out of my four grandparents were fat; my parents are fat. Even when I was a small, slender child, I could feel the impending threat of the familial curse. And the harpies are also associated, in stories, with food: The harpies harass people while they eat, flying into banquet halls, snatching the food off the tables, then befouling the rest of the food, making it inedible. As fat people know, an obsession with weight can make food itself a disgusting, even terrifying, sight.

The Harpy screeched at me, night and day, "You are an ugly failure, and will remain so, until you lose the Weight." Some people think of it as "thirty pounds" or "getting down to a size seven" but for me it was always just "the Weight." The Weight was not an actual thing—the fat on my body, as always, was not the real issue—it was a weight of self-deprecation, within my mind. It was as if the Weight didn't exist, until the Harpy began to harp on me.

She rarely left me any peace. She had an unerring memory and could at any time recite a complete list of all my failures. She could produce at a moment's notice a chart detailing the ups and downs in my weight over the years. She attached numbers to important occasions in my life: when I went to college the number was 134, when I began professional training, 151, and so on. She maddened me with these numbers, as if all my achievements were in vain if that three-digit figure weren't the right one. As the years went by, the voice of the Harpy remarkably followed me from one phase of my life to another; that voice was the only constant during a period in which my mental and emotional development were proceeding apace.

Yet, with time, that vociferousness began to threaten the Harpy's position. She drew too much attention to herself. A shadowy entity is always threatened by self-awareness. The monster is more threatening when you can't quite perceive it. As soon as you become fully, consciously aware that you're harboring such a beast in your head, the battle is joined. This point was, I'm sure of it, when I began to change. Once I could see the Harpy clearly, I began to differentiate what I considered to be my true self from her incessantly critical voice. That key step of recognition made her pronouncements less believable.

During this period of consciousness-raising, I started reading books about my dilemma. I found startling ideas, for example, in Susie Orbach's *Fat is a Feminist Issue*. Two revelations arrived like twins: being fat has advantages, and being thin has disadvantages. When you're fat, you're big, you take up space, you're solid. When you're thin, you may feel pinched, vulnerable, or lacking in warmth. When you're fat, you are often perceived as a generous person, a person with ample resources. When you're thin, other people may look at you in envy, or in dismay, for you activate the critical voices that reside in other women's minds. I found myself asking, as Orbach coached me to do, "What about this scene would be different if I were thin? What if I were much fatter?" Such simple concepts—but the Harpy's screeching hadn't let me hear them.

I think of this phase as a phase of gathering data. I started collecting positive images of fat people. Such images are few and far between in our society, but you can find them if you look. When Nelson Mandela was released from prison, the news showed footage of fat women dancing with abandon, dancing exuberantly in the streets of South Africa. I saw for the first time that fat can mean freedom. Books about ancient religions showed picture after picture of fat women worshipped as the great creatrix, the mother of all things. I saw for the first time that fat can mean power. Gunter Grass' novel *The Flounder* sang praises to the ample bottom, with its "one hundred and eleven dimples," of the mighty Awa, a heroically large and giving (three-breasted) ruler of a fictional Stone Age. I saw for the first time the connection that was hardest of all to grasp—that fat can mean beauty.

The Harpy remained, though. She seemed, in fact, to grow more and more persistent as I grew older. I could see that the Harpy had lost all credibility. I could see that the Harpy was not me. Around that time my little sister dieted and exercised her way down to her desired weight. When she told me about crying in front of the mirror, because losing weight had not magically made her a gorgeous, glamorous person, I realized, "I don't need to lose weight to learn this lesson." Yet in another part of me, I was still enslaved to the inner monster. For all my new-found reasoning, I was figuring out new ways to run myself down. Through a clever loop of self-defeating logic, I told myself that the fact I still listened to those irrational messages about my weight was further proof of what a useless person I was. The older I got, the more heinous it seemed to me that the Harpy controlled me. If I were so free and feminist, if I were really older and wiser as I claimed to be, why hadn't I liberated myself from this creature?

I stayed stuck at this point for a long time.

I imagine that many women reading this book are stuck at this point. You know, rationally, that the quest to attain slenderness is more trouble than it's worth, and even that it's not consistent with your hard-won values about how a woman should live, but you can't quite believe that fat is beautiful. You can't hold on to your sense of how your inner world could be differently put together. When you close the book, when you walk up to your clothes closet, the reasoning mind drops away; and the Harpy returns to harass you.

I hope that for others, the final step in the process will be easier, but for me, it took a major crisis—a clinical depression. In the summer of my thirty-third year, I succumbed to a severe mood disorder. I struggled for months to maintain my life, but eventually, I lost my job, my self-respect, my very sense of hope for the future. My awareness shrunk to an oppressive grey box filled with crushing fatigue, self-defeating thoughts of a numbing intensity, and never-ceasing psychological pain. I landed, after a long slide through money worries and disappointment, medications and doctors' offices, in a one-bedroom apartment in Houston, Texas. There, every day, I sat in a chair by a window, staring out into an urban garden, watching banana plants grow. And it was there, in a position of such severe pain that I had no choice but to work very hard to learn the negative patterns in my head and unravel them, that my relationship with the Harpy began to change.

This process was akin to being tortured into doing something. I don't lay claim to any great courage—I was forced into it by overwhelming circumstance. Simply to crawl my way out of the pain, I had to work with my thoughts according to a new set of rules. I sat in that chair by the window and taught myself, little by little, to ignore exaggerated pronouncements about what a failure I was. I learned to look for places where I was thinking more positively about my life, to concentrate on expanding them. Through this process of slowly retraining my thoughts, almost inadvertently I began to apply these rules to my thinking about the weight issue. The Harpy, the Weight—those entities didn't mean much to me in the depth of my despair—and because they didn't mean much, I didn't think of them as separate from all my other negative thoughts. All those self-castigating messages were in the same container, and my very future depended on cleaning out that container.

Not that the forces of my depression didn't often ally themselves with the Harpy—the daily defeats before my clothes closet, for example, got even worse. I had an awkward, overstuffed closet—a poorly made wardrobe that jutted out into the room and was covered with mirror tiles. What could be worse for someone who felt herself irreversibly ugly? The wardrobe had a folding door that was difficult to manage without things getting caught in it. I'd wrestle with the door, and jam it on a piece of clothing, and suddenly the clothes caught in the door seemed as disgusting to me as food between my teeth or toilet paper on my shoe.

But a bitter, no-nonsense force lay behind my survival instincts at that time. Nothing, absolutely nothing, was as important to me as finding an end to the pain. No other inner struggle could compare in magnitude to the battle to heal my psyche and recover from depression. I became ruthless in my quest to reduce stress in my life. I found myself capable, for example, of exiting from situations that previously would have controlled me. Social occasions, grocery shopping, driving to the bank—in midstream, if I felt I could no longer tolerate the situation, I would pull a mental ripcord, and return to the safety of my chair before the window.

When I applied this same ruthless reasoning to the things the Harpy had always told me about my body—that I was an unsightly mess, that I would never amount to anything if I didn't lose weight—those thoughts became yet another stressful situation I had to escape from. The Harpy's messages did have a much longer history in my mind, thus they were more securely entrenched than the negative thoughts arising from my depression. Once I saw these thoughts begin to erode, and I compared the awakening pleasures in my life to the ongoing onus of that clothes closet with its silly mirrors, I had a surge of hope I'd never had before, hope about getting a handle on the fat issue. The depression had affected me much the same way people describe being affected by a heart attack. It caused me to reevaluate everything so thoroughly, nothing could ever be the same again, even that old standby—the Harpy.

The banana plants grew to two-story height in the garden, my depression receded, and the changes I experienced during convalescence and its aftermath swept away the Harpy like so much flotsam in a flood. I discovered new magazines for women who celebrate their fatness. I bought new clothes, which still fit, much to my amazement. I felt a new freedom of movement and more physical energy than I'd ever had, even before the depression. Best of all, I welcomed a whole new freedom within my own mind. With the Harpy defeated at last, I am no longer afraid of my own thoughts. I have more room in there—an odd sensation, as if a constricting labyrinth has turned into a wide open countryside. I have more room to think about my self-worth, more room to plan my future.

I wonder, these days, about how other women find their self-acceptance—whether it's easier for others than it was for me, or whether it's even harder. I wonder about how to help spread what feels like a "good news" story. I've concluded that acceptance of one's body is such a key step in the maturation of a woman that it must take place at some point, no matter what she weighs.

I believe that if a woman loses weight in an effort to achieve that acceptance, she will discover that the battle with her own Harpy is still waiting for her, on the other side of the weight loss. The wisest among us, the crones, the older women, have been saying this for years: Sexual attractiveness need not be defined by society, and self-worth need not be defined by sexual attractiveness. I believe this step into self-acceptance never comes without a struggle, that it doesn't come automatically, even to the most beautiful of us. Perhaps those of us who are fat are lucky, because we are forced to become the heroines of our own life-adventures at a younger age than others.

Perhaps I should thank the Harpy, now that she's dead.

Barbara Elder

No Skinny Jeans!

Barbara Elder

Today I threw out my "skinny jeans." I went through my closet, and in a fit of self-love and reckless abandon, stripped myself of every skirt, blouse, and pair of jeans that I'd been saving for that long-awaited day when I finally lost weight. You know the jeans I'm talking about. Maybe you have a pair in your closet. Maybe you were able to wear them at one time. Or maybe you've never put them on, but merely bought them as a clever diet incentive. Whatever their history, there they are, in the back of almost every closet, the skinny jeans—reeking of dust and mildew, and carrying an aura of willpower, good intentions, and lost hopes.

I planned on someday wearing mine. I was going to buy a halter top or something to go with those skinny jeans, something to show off my belly button. I was going to wear them in public and wiggle my skinny butt. I was going to be thin and beautiful and sexy and socially acceptable.

But today I threw them out, along with the size-twelve leather mini-skirt and the skin-tight, low-cut Frederick's of Hollywood blouse. Gone, garbage, tossed, exit, *fini*, no more.

What happened? Why the sudden skinny purge? I got angry. Angry at a lot of things. I had been, for some time, angry at myself for failing at all those diets, for failing to be perfect and beautiful and skinny and socially acceptable. But then I noticed that things outside myself were making me feel this way.

It started when I realized how much I hated the beach. I'd been living in a beach town for two years and had yet to go down to sunbathe or swim in the ocean. I realized that I was very angry about this. I was angry at all the so-called beautiful people, the skinny, busty creatures bouncing around in their bikinis, playing volleyball with all the well-muscled, skinny men in their Speedo swim trunks. I was jealous of their bare flesh and their lack of embarrassment. And I was angry at the scornful looks they would give me, as I marched by on my way to drown my sorrows in calimari. I would pull my voluminous garb tighter around me to shield my body from their stares.

Most of the anger would come as I watched these skinny beach people pile into their beautiful beachmobiles, their shiny cars with the surfboards on top, the ones with bumper stickers that said "No Fat Chicks." It was finally that, the sticker, that made me angrier than anything else. I am still angry when I think of it. Would these same bigots dare to put stickers on their cars that read "No African-Americans" or "No Mexican-Americans"?

What gave them the right to blatantly, publicly insult a large (pun intended) part of the population? What gave them the right to insult *me*?

But then I realized that I was giving them that right. I gave it to them by hiding my body in clothes that made me unhappy and ugly. I gave them the power to hurt me when I avoided their beaches, heightening our "differentness." I gave them power over me by not telling them they were wrong. Because I thought, deep down, that they were right—that I was ugly and socially unacceptable, that I shouldn't look the way I did, and that they had every right to criticize me. But how can hurting another human being be right? How can self-loathing and insulting be right? How can forced torture such as dieting be right?

Anger, anger, anger. And for the first time, not at myself. At "Them." At all of those who have made being heavy an emotional load to bear. And, finally, I realized that I was, deep down, one of Them. I was one of Them when I saw myself as ugly, unsexy, unimportant, unworthy.

I don't want to be part of that kind of anger and hatred anymore. I don't want to be part of Them. I want to be Us and We. I decided to stop looking at my body as something wrong that needed to be fixed. I decided that I would wear beautiful clothes. I would wiggle my Fat Chick butt. I am sexy. Sexy shines through everything. It is personality, not body, that makes sexy. Lots of skinny women have low self-esteem and no lovers.

And yes, I go to the beach. And I make love with the lights on. I don't suck my tummy in anymore when my lover looks at my body. He is there to make love to me—my mind, my soul, and every cushy curve I've got. It's me he's with, not one of Them.

Make no mistake, I still have to work at it. Sometimes I just need to do something small to remind myself that I don't have to be a slave to Them anymore. Like throwing out all of my skinny clothes today. I was still harboring a little anger. Not much, just a little. I was angry because all those skinny clothes were taking up valuable closet space. I have large-size lingerie to put on that shelf and beautiful blouses to hang on those hooks.

As the skinny jeans hit the garbage bag with a satisfying plastic hiss, I smiled. A chubby, dimpled, cheerful, thank-God-I'm-finally-free kind of smile.

A Change of Heart: How I Learned to Stop Hating Myself and Others

Katharine Schneider

As a child I fantasized about being able to divorce my body at will, my "self" leaving my body behind, perhaps hidden in the closet or under the blankets at the foot of my bed. The world this bodiless self would inhabit was a world of freedom, of weightlessness. A world where I wasn't judged by the size of my body but by the mind and soul that was my true self.

This fantasy was most vivid when I lay on my bed after school, perhaps eating a bag of chocolate chips or white bread with mayonnaise, swallowing with it the confused shame that dominated my self-awareness. Days of homemade polyester stretch pants and oversized blouses; mumbled excuses for not showering after physical education; boys chanting in time with my steps down the hallway, "Fat-ty! Fat-ty-fat-ty-fat-ty!" or steering wide arcs around me as they walked by, exaggerating the true size of my body; torturous walks home, losing track of the insults hurled out car windows.

My spirit world overcame me when relatives came to visit. I overheard their loud whispers in the other room: ". . . getting so fat . . . mother doing to her? . . . go on a diet before . . ." My father's family, thin and obsessed with not getting fat. My mother, fat and obsessed with getting thin.

And me, learning it was right to hate my body because it was not thin, learning it was wrong to lie in the bathtub and appreciate the way my belly arched out of the water. My school friend and I, sleeping over at each other's houses, would lie awake at night and take turns pretending we had a magic knife and describing which parts of our flesh we would cut into and off. Or we would hope out loud that someday we could each take a pill that would transform us into gaunt models.

My mother had a special cupboard in the kitchen. This cupboard became more crowded each time my mother ran for a pen and paper to scribble down a phone number flashing on the television screen, "Lose all the weight you want and still eat hamburgers and sundaes! That's right! Money-back guarantee! Call 1-800- . . ." My mother would roll off the couch, furiously repeating the number until she could write it down. Each new product she ordered she threw into the cupboard with the rest (candy to suppress that "uncontrollable" appetite; little sponges that swelled, filling that "bottomless" stomach; magic powders to mix with milk and drink three times a day to melt that "unsightly" fat) after a few days of no miraculous results. Invariably, these disappointments were followed by long days of eating, until self-hatred propelled her to scribble down yet another number.

The family physician said it was "shameful" to let me get so fat and for my mother to be so fat herself. Like a good doctor, he conjured up a little white pill, a miracle of modern medicine, that would tame the beasts of our hunger once and for all. The result: sudden and prolonged hours of weeping, my eyes swollen almost shut; sweaty jitters during class; my craving to take more and more of those little white pills. Finally, those little white pills ended up in the back of my mother's cupboard with everything else.

At the age when my voice raised a pitch and I became giggly and silly interacting with the opposite sex, I met a boy in my typing class. He never knew how he inspired me. I began looking up the calorie content of a celery stalk, eating it, and then recording it in my daily log; weighing that chicken breast (four ounces exactly) on the food scale I had saved money to buy; berating myself when the bathroom scale needle didn't point to a lower number each morning; and further lowering my calorie intake, overlooking the clumps of hair that ended up in my brush each day and keeping secret the fainting spells that tumbled me to the ground, in slow motion, when I stood up too fast. Why, I was going to make myself thin. I was going to make him notice me.

I watched Miss America pageants and the women on soap operas and in television advertisements. This was how I was supposed to look.

The boy in the typing class never noticed me, and the needle on the bathroom scale pointed to ever higher numbers just as quickly as it had previously dropped to lower numbers. This process of weight loss and regain repeated itself many times throughout the next several years of my life.

After some years of hoping and trying, I finally gave up on remolding my body or escaping my body. I began to grapple with the reality of being in my body. Tired of despising thin women for their thin bodies, tired of despising fat women for mirroring back to me my own body, tired of despising men for creating these unreal ideals of womanhood, tired of feeling alienated, I decided to make friends with at least one person: myself.

My change of heart might have begun the night I danced naked in the dark. Or maybe it started the morning I let myself get undressed and take a shower without turning on the cacophony of critical voices in my head. Or when I befriended a thin woman who shared many similar body worries. Or the first time I let myself eat a pint of ice cream and enjoy it. Perhaps the changes all began the evening I suddenly felt compelled to let my body speak. I got out a piece of paper and a pen and scribbled furiously. All the pain and oppression and torturous silence my body had had to bear for so many years—the pain of not being trusted, the pain of not being used, the pain of being fed beyond fullness, the pain of being starved—all came screaming out. And we cried—my body, my spirit, my mind—until we became one.

Looking back, I realize that the internalized oppression I was living with had been learned over many years and that freeing myself from it has been a long, patient, daily struggle. Since I began this process, I have discovered new courage and pleasure in the world around me.

Some of the most beautiful things I've witnessed: Five fat women sitting in an ice cream parlor, napkins tucked into their blouses, eating ravenously, laughing, dribbling ice cream from a huge shared dish to their mouths. A fat woman walking briskly down the street in the afternoon sun, waving and smiling to the person in a passing car who made a comment about her size. A fat woman asking the waiter in a restaurant to find her a large chair. A group of fat women sharing frustrations, encouragement, and their journeys of self-acceptance. A fat woman dancing, her round hips swaying, breasts swinging. The way my belly gracefully arches out of the warm water of my bath.

Patricia Cominos

Journey to Self-Acceptance

Patricia Cominos

When I began to become fat in my eleventh year, my father joked that it was the mountain air. He had moved us to the country, about 120 miles from New York City. This move suited me just fine, because I loved climbing trees and stalking the hilly woods behind our rented house.

I would take my little ten-cent corncob pipe, fill it with crushed dry leaves, light it with a pilfered kitchen match, and view the world from the nook of some comfortable old tree limb. Life was good. Even when we moved to the other end of town, there were plenty of trees and an entirely new wooded area behind the house to explore.

One day I was playing in the clay banks along the creek with my best and cutest friend, Dicky. He made some little remark about weight, but I took only slight notice at the time. That night, though, while getting ready for bed, I began to see and feel the extra flesh that had accumulated on my body. I shrugged it off and decided to punch Dicky if he ever bugged me about it again.

Then, while sitting at my desk in the sixth grade, behind Dicky, my world was sucked away. Dicky was surrounded by a group of boys, one of whom was teasing him about our long relationship, which we both considered a special kind of buddy thing, even though I was a girl. Then, it happened. Dicky said, "Who? Fatty Patty? I don't like her." Then he sang, "She's too fat for me."

From that moment I was obsessed with my weight. I let Dicky Algozzine define me, as a girl, as a human being, on into womanhood. I was Fatty Patty. The more obsessed I became about my weight, the bigger I got. Then, the next year, I broke my leg in three places while ice skating. I was confined (with a heavy cast up to my hip) to a wheelchair and the daybed in the living room. My father owned a small diner, and to make his "little" girl feel better, he brought her fried chicken, ice cream, pie, and you-name-it, I got it. I ballooned up to 160 pounds and peaked at 175 in my senior year.

Like many fat people, I found humor to be a saving grace. I had many friends, some who really knew me, and some who just got a kick out of my wise remarks, especially those bravely tossed out in the constricted class-room atmosphere of pre-revolutionary high school days.

I coped, even while desperately trying to turn some forty-year-old's housedress into a wearable frock. In those days, we weren't allowed to wear anything but dresses or skirts to school, and the clothing available to "large" girls and women added insult to injury. Society heaped us together in large bundles of "fat and dowdy."

I laughed and drank my way through high school; I had only one se-nior prom to humiliate me. At all our high school dances, I was the disc jockey. Occasionally, a buddy danced with me, but there was no romance.

Just out of school, I decided I'd had enough. I starved myself and lost fifty pounds in three months. The following summer, I hit the local bars with some of my friends who were home from college. What a thrill it was the first time a man approached me. Until then, during a night out with the girls, I had always been abandoned (at least temporarily) by friends for some "better offer." Well, the thrill of being approached, dated, or even made love to didn't last long. At the age of eighteen, I realized that a de-cent-looking body was not a cure-all. Slowly, the weight crept back, along with an extra ten pounds.

In my twenties, I bought into society's judgment of fat people as lazy weaklings, though in my heart I knew better. I decided to show my strength of will by doing Dr. Stillman's protein diet. I lost fifty-five pounds and kept them off for three years.

Then, one night, while lying on the couch in my apartment, I rediscov-ered myself. Dressed in my pajamas, I casually ran my hand down over my stomach. A peculiar sense of loss struck me. It was not the same con-crete sense of loss I felt when my father died. I had been fifteen at the time, and I remember his death as a huge gaping void, though I had watched him slowly turn to dust for seven years. He had been a large man, an Army cook during World War II, but in the last years of his life, he wasted away in his illness. He died thin.

In the year before my revelation, my mother, who had been a stout, handsome, hard-working woman, also died thin, of colon cancer. That loss was also concrete, and my feelings then were deep and sorrowful, but not at all peculiar, like the feeling that came over me that night on the couch.

I remember thinking, "God, what have I done? I've given away a part of my self to please whom?" And at the same time, "You're much better off thinner, you know, healthwise and all." But that loss, that torn part of me called out louder than all other thoughts. I had reached a turning point. I had just completed two years of college, finally escaped the repression of an utterly life-stifling relationship (one that I, then unconsciously, felt a fat, lazy person probably deserved), and met someone who genuinely loved me. No doubt a combination of academic achievement, artistic achievement (I had some poems published in a small literary journal), my new friend, and self-love turned the tide.

I have regained the weight, plus some, but I have never, in the eighteen years since, seriously thought about dieting. I work out at a gym twice a week to keep my blood sugar level and blood pressure normal. The exercise keeps me from having to take medication, keeps my large body toned, and keeps me feeling better all over. I keep an eye on my food choices so that they're not madly fattening. I do not deliberately diet. I will never again.

More and more information is coming out now about yo-yo dieting and genetic predisposition toward weight gain. We who are fat have "known" these things for most of our lives. We are not lazy. We can be strong-willed people. Most of us have proven it by getting by on little, if any, food for days and weeks on end, time after time on diets throughout our lives. We now need to recognize that it is not our duty to create a visually thin and thereby "inoffensive" world for those thin-prejudiced people. Our duty is to create a healthy, happy, and loving environment for ourselves. I now feel comfortable and secure tucking in my shirts and walking in my shorts. I take special pleasure in beginning each day with the sweet, soft feeling of my body sliding under my soap-lathered hands in the shower.

Bernadette Lynn Bosky

Some Painful and Healing Words

Bernadette Lynn Bosky

At 5'4" tall and consistently weighing between 265 and 285 pounds, I am "fat" by anyone's standards. In this culture, almost anyone my size will be preoccupied with it, as almost anyone with dark skin will be preoccupied with that, because it is stigmatized, not because it is inherently important. Fortunately, I can choose to be preoccupied in a self-hating way, or in a positive way, using my concern, empathy, and righteous anger to heal myself and reach out to others. I actually now spend far less time researching, writing, and speaking about size issues than I used to spend feeling bad, looking forward to when I would be "thin enough" to feel better. Perhaps it seems like more, because I am accomplishing something and can feel the progress.

I just turned thirty-six years old. For half those years, my life was dominated by watching my weight and dieting—alternating periods of guilty eating and calorie restriction, which meant a small mountain range of rises and falls in my weight. Before I gave up dieting, seven years ago, I had never worn the same dress size for more than three years, often less.

I was aware of calories when I was ten years old or younger. Offered a Popsicle at a friend's house, I wondered if I could "afford" the calories. The question had nothing to do with hunger or taste; I was already thinking of food in terms of what I could get away with. Not surprisingly, this was often linked to trickery and guilt: I decided to eat the Popsicle by giving up the equivalent calories in two non-diet Coca-Colas, which I probably would not have had anyway. I felt a sting of shame at pulling this scam on myself—which I'm sure is why the memory is so strong—but it seemed the only way to make the equation work out the way I wanted it to.

I was not officially on a diet then, but the goals and methods were clearly part of my family culture. I remember my father going to evening meetings that had something to do with weight. Decades later, going through his papers after his death, I found literature from TOPS—Take Off Pounds Sensibly, a precursor of Weight Watchers—and made the connection. The meetings were in the building where he worked, and I'm sure his company encouraged him to sign up.

My mother's relationship with weight and eating influenced me in an even deeper and more complex way. From her I learned the basics about "good" and "bad" foods, both the overt rules of nutrition and the covert message that the bad foods were most desirable, especially in times of stress. Both "overweight" and diabetic, she would ostentatiously eat sweets after family arguments, symbolically and often literally saying that we made her do it by upsetting her.

I know I learned the worst message about weight from my mother: that "fat" and "pretty" were two incompatible categories. Although I now feel hatred and rage at that message, I don't blame my mother for passing it on. If she hadn't, I would have learned it from my school-mates—and the shock might have been even more rude. Mostly, she taught me what she had been taught, and that belief cost her much more than it cost me. I am as angry *for* my mother, who was often beautiful (at any weight) but could not see it, as I could ever be *at* her. And didn't I believe the same thing, just as fervently, through all my years of dieting?

The aesthetic condemnation of fat wasn't taught explicitly and didn't have to be. It was assumed, and all judgments and advice proceeded from there. My mother would show me a picture of herself on horseback, during college, and say, "Didn't I look good, then?" Perhaps she meant her smile, her enthusiasm, the proud way she sat; certainly, she meant she was thinner.

When I began to diet during high school, appealing to possible boy-friends was the major carrot (or perhaps celery stick) held out to motivate me: slender=pretty= desirable=dates. I saw that evidence in my sisters, ten and eight years older. One was slender and always had her opportunities; most importantly, my oldest sister lost some weight in college and only then became the center of a social whirl of men—or so it seemed to me. Later, my younger sister dated when I did not, which I attributed primarily to her weighing less than I did (and hence being "prettier").

These sad "facts" about fat and attractiveness were reinforced outside my family. I especially remember one bittersweet interaction in high school. Noticing that I was unhappy about romance, a high school debate coach opened up to me personally, heard me out, and offered advice: Perhaps I could lose weight, as she had the year before, gaining a new boyfriend. The memory brings conflicting feelings—gratitude that she would reach out to me, anger at the culture that left her with only one suggestion for how to look good. I sometimes replay that conversation, thinking of all the other possibilities in an alternate world that would have been far better for both of us.

At least my upbringing was generally free of the verbal abuse so many fat adolescents get, especially in my own family. Still, some comments hurt, usually statements about the attractiveness that could be mine if I lost weight. I remember only one, presumably the worst. I was growing my hair long and for the first time could pull it back in a bun. "When you lose weight," said my mother to "encourage" me, "you'll look like Doris Day when you do that, instead of Horrible Katrinka." I didn't know who Horrible Katrinka was and didn't think Doris Day looked all that great, but the message was clear, and I accepted it unquestioningly. The worst part was that I had felt I looked good. Had I managed to momentarily forget that I was too heavy to ever look really good?

My family was supportive in many other ways, and in my adolescence I never doubted that I would be "a real knock-out" if I lost weight. That is, slenderness was necessary for looking good, but not sufficient; I qualified in other ways, however, so all I had to do was diet.

To this I dedicated myself, epitomizing the combined fervor and ignorance of the time. The myth was that once I reached the appropriate weight, "sensible eating" would maintain it. My stomach, "stretched" from my presumed gluttony, would "shrink" back, so I would not be hungry. It was as though some force of nature would have kept my body at the insurance-chart weights, except that I willfully upset the balance with what and how much I ate. Though I had no idea how it would work, I assumed that once I reached my "right" weight, this force would again kick in. In reality, I went from an adolescence of watching my weight to major dieting; three times I lost twenty pounds or more, with a high of seventy-five. Each time I regained what I had lost and more, in cycles of three to five years.

I never reached my goal weight, although the last time, when calorie watching plus two hours of exercise a day brought me down to 165 pounds, I was almost willing to settle for that. Ironically, when I had begun worrying about weight, the scale had shown the unacceptable reading of (you guessed it) 165 pounds. Though I'd grown to my full height by then, I was young, and I'm sure that wouldn't be my natural weight now; but without the weight increases after major diets, I don't think I'd be my current weight either. I'll never know for certain, but to the extent that the "problem" may have created itself—which I think is likely—I don't know whether to laugh or cry.

Still, each stage of my history of weight fluctuation has provided a step or two on the path to self-acceptance. Yes, even the diets. I could have learned the same lessons in other ways, I'm sure, at less physical and emotional cost, but you take what you can get.

In college, for instance, I put myself on calorie restrictions that (I hope) would now be viewed as pathological: consistently under 1000 calories a day, I often kept myself below 500. My friends and the housemother saw me, but they knew nothing about eating disorders. (It might not have changed things if they had, but I'd like to think it would have.) I was praised for my self-control and successful weight loss. Years later, I would write to myself, "When anorexia works, they call it dieting."

My rigidly controlled eating and fat-phobic attitudes resembled those of anorexics but worked in two ways. From the outside, everything seemed okay, because I had a "weight problem" and was ready to stop when I reached the "right" weight. Most importantly—and I do literally thank God for it—dieting itself gave me the satisfaction and pride that allowed me to stop. I felt a need to assert myself, to prove something about being in control. I also needed to win something from others, and all the words for that—acceptance, attraction, praise—came down to one word, love. These words were not clear at the time, but the needs were. With each hunger pang, I felt more self-control. With each pound shed, I felt—and was treated as—more lovable.

I can imagine what it would be like not to get those feelings, or not to get enough, or not to be able to accept that one has gotten them—and hence not to stop "dieting" because the needs are not met. I don't know if this possibility existed for me then, but the idea scares and saddens me.

Even as I regained the weight, I retained some of the feelings of love and control, and the knowledge that I could win these when I tried. I also reinforced my rejection of my body, learned to make weight even more central in my life, and felt empowered to pass along the myths of weight and dieting even more fervently. But the good feelings stayed with me, every bit as much as the bad ones (and the lowered metabolism and increased setpoint).

Dieting also helped me learn certain kinds of physical pleasure, especially simple joy of movement. This would not be necessary if fat people were taught pride in our bodies, but until recently I could hardly imagine that such joy and pride could be, let alone what it would be like. While fat people may be overtly told we should exercise, we are covertly discouraged from doing so in many ways, from lack of appropriate clothes in large sizes to outright derision when we are active. (Calisthenics are mocked somewhat less, seen as an unpleasant but necessary part of losing weight.) My physical education classes alone taught me that there was no point in exercise, and I certainly should not enjoy myself, unless I was going to lose some weight. The gym teacher was fat, and only later did I understand the pushing-around and name-calling—"chunko," "elephant," the ironic "Miss America"—as perverted outgrowths of his own shame.

The gospels of physical culture and weight loss were as one. During grade school, I took weekly acrobatic lessons. These exacting, three-hour lessons epitomized both messages: the joys and freedom of a cartwheel and worries about "getting fat"; the self-control of stretches and backbends and comments that showed my eating was carefully monitored. In college, a friend taught me yoga, and we exercised together to lose weight; I also learned to enjoy movement—and simple physical being—in new and exciting ways. It's pitiful I felt I had to be thin (or working on it) to learn certain truths about the wonders of the body, but it was a blessing that I glimpsed those truths at all.

Physical movement has been the hardest aspect of self-love for me to cultivate without dieting. Part of me still sees exercise as a chore or even, perhaps, a punishment; and I don't have much experience with physically strenuous activities apart from exercise. Yet I have learned a simple joy in everyday activities—including walking and even breathing—that I denied myself before, or didn't know existed. I enjoy playing badminton and learning T'ai Chi. And sometimes I dance, just for myself.

By the time my weight was rebounding from my last diet, I had begun to hear about "fat liberation" and read the new findings about metabolism and setpoint. I was not ready to fully challenge society's (and my own) condemnations of fat, but I was immediately fascinated and convinced by the scientific research. Setpoint was almost the opposite of the "shrinking stomach" and "sensible eating" school: The body does have homeostatic mechanisms, but they preserve fat. As calorie intake goes down, energy use slows, making weight loss more difficult and encouraging future production of fat. All of this makes sense from an evolutionary viewpoint. Only recently has starvation been deliberate, instead of a sign that food supply is unstable and more fat may mean survival.

The information was compelling, and I was ready for it. The last diet had been everything it could be: I'd eaten a balanced diet of natural foods, not a crash diet like the one in college. I had exercised in ways that made me feel better physically and emotionally. I had thought seriously about the need to maintain the weight loss, although I had no idea how. I had not cheated, and I had not been too extreme. By all standards, my diet had been impeccable. Now this research suggested the fault could lie with dieting itself. I concluded that if calorie reduction could work for me, this diet would have.

The new "anti-diet" literature gave me the courage to give up dieting, based on statements that the body has its own weight, or setpoint. This setpoint will fluctuate somewhat, due to a number of factors (notably physical activity), but the tendency is to stay the same. Beyond explaining the flaw in calorie-reduction dieting, setpoint theory also implied that if I ate naturally (in accord with my own hunger), I wouldn't lose weight, but I wouldn't go on gaining forever, either. I didn't believe that emotionally, but it seemed sound intellectually, and I made it an article of faith. I swore, like Scarlett at Tara, that "with God as my witness, I'll never be hungry again!"

Outwardly, that last weight regain was no different from the others; inside, I was terrified, knowing I'd vowed not to stop the process by dieting but fearing it might not ever stop without dieting. After all, dieting also teaches that food is powerful and hunger must be controlled, that without willpower we'd all be big as houses. My spouse joked me through the hard times. "Do you think I'll just keep gaining weight forever," I asked him, "like the chicken heart in that radio play? Until I take over the whole Earth?" No, he'd reassure me, "Oh, I doubt you'll get any bigger than a city block." (You might have to know and maybe share our sense of humor, but that genuinely was reassuring.) It sounds like disordered thinking—and I believe it literally is—but there it was. Against the fear was the support of my spouse, evidence from some scientific studies, and my own mule-stubborn inner commitment to become as good at loving myself as I am as I had been at dieting.

Seven years later, the fear is gone, at least most of the time. Sometimes, when I feel low, I become convinced that I have gained weight—but I am sane enough to apply and accept a reality check, panicked enough to be surprised that my clothes still fit in the same way. (I used to step on my scale, but when the scale broke, fixing it seemed more effort than it was worth.) I continue to learn how much my body image can be grounded in my fears, doubts, and guilt rather than in reality; and I continue to be saddened by this, for myself and others.

My oldest sister is now a recovering anorexic, and for all the ways in which we are almost opposites (including our places on the natural bell-curve of body weight), I feel I understand some of her problems all too well. My hatred of my "thunder thighs" and her anorexic desire for a flat stomach (still not achieved when she reached 110 pounds, at a height of over 5'8") seem to be part of the same continuum, or at least to share some essential pathology.

For some, food can be an addiction. It is for compulsive eaters, as my oldest sister was before she became anorexic. I think it may have been for me, at some time during my adolescence. In some ways, dieting helped me feel less compelled by food and less likely to eat past satiation. By the time I regained weight after the last diet, however, my addiction clearly was not food, but dieting. I felt I needed dieting to "be okay," yet it never delivered what it promised. And it colored even my most basic thoughts. Feeling bad because you are "fat" is bad enough; it is far worse to also "feel fat" when you are unhappy. These cultural prejudices are so powerful they distort your natural self-perception.

In another way, it is liberating to realize how much our self-concept, even something as seemingly objective as body size, is "socially constructed." What the psyche constructs, it can deconstruct (in Derrida's sense or otherwise) and, most importantly, reconstruct. I know that much of my quest to accept myself as I am is essentially self-brainwashing. I have moments of doubt: What am I doing? What if I'm convincing myself of something totally wrong? Yet it's undeniable that my weight has not continued to rise, and my self-esteem has. Undeniably, I am more likely to like what I see in the mirror now than I was at my lowest adult weight, 100 or so pounds lighter. And the more I feel righteous anger about what I've been through, working it through in productive ways, the happier I am.

One important part of this process is what I call "clothes-buying therapy." Paradoxically, I benefited because Durham, North Carolina (from which I recently moved) is a major diet center: The dieters have to buy new clothes, many still in large sizes. As a result, the shopping mall nearest me had four large-size clothes stores, with others elsewhere in Durham. If plus-size clothing shops had provided that much variety, quality, and style when I was growing up, how different things might have been! I know it's still possible to buy the officially sanctioned flattering clothes, the "minimizing" dark colors and shapeless cuts "to hide figure flaws." Fortunately it's also possible to buy other clothes, flattering in the true sense: well-made, well-fitting, appropriate to one's own personality and proportions. I had begun to appreciate this before my final diet; afterward, it became vital.

If I can locate my turnabout concerning weight and self-acceptance in one moment, it was as I tried on clothes in the store. I must have started out discouraged, because last year's outfits no longer fit. However, as I tried on a summer suit—white, with large blue cabbage roses—and looked at myself in the mirror, I thought, "Wow. This looks pretty good." In fact, *I* looked pretty good. Maybe, I thought, this could work.

Some relay had been tripped—from thinking about how I should look, to thinking about how I did and could look; from hoping to make the body fit the clothes, to demanding clothes that fit the body. I also began a process, long and difficult but always worthwhile, of seeing myself in a more accepting (and perhaps more realistic) way, focusing on the whole instead of harshly scrutinizing each part.

I bought that suit and some other clothes that fit and looked good. I also made a new resolve, enacted as soon as I got home: I will never again keep in my closet or drawers any clothes that I cannot wear (and look great in) at my present weight. I still have dreams in which I have an important appointment, but any appropriate items in my closet are too small. I wake and think, "Ha! I used to *live* like that!" In reality, my clothes closet is ten feet long and full of clothes, *all of which fit me.* I'm lucky to have enough money for my "clothes-horse school of self-esteem"; still, I'm always amazed by how much money I have for frivolous clothes, now that I'm not rebuying the basics every year or three. Instead of a source of shame and oppression, clothes have become a source of joy, and a means of expressing aspects of my life and self.

I also surround myself with positive fat images, a collection ranging from prints of Renaissance paintings to catalogs for large-size lingerie, from reproductions of Paleolithic goddess-sculptures to refrigerator magnets in the shape of smiling, anthropomorphic fat cats. I treasure drawings and sculpture that show realistic human bodies, of any size, in all their extravagantly different proportions. I study the outward swell of belly here, or the double-chin there, often recorded more faithfully in a less air-brushed age than ours. Recently, I startled a woman who overheard me commenting on the female figure in a water-globe I was buying: "She's not fat enough, but she does have a lovely double chin." I don't think that a large, rounded figure is inherently beautiful, but it's wonderful to learn how often it can be. I now laugh at New Age drawings in which an Earth Goddess, symbolic of fecundity and grandeur, has a body as "perfect" and petite as a fashion model.

In the past few years something interesting has happened to my aesthetic sense, dramatic in practice but hard to explain in theory. I no longer automatically perceive people who lose weight as better looking. I can think of two people who were significantly more appealing to me—part of it was their happiness, energy, and pride, which could perhaps have been achieved without the change in size; but there seemed to be something else, having to do with contours and movement. On the other hand, at least one person seemed significantly less good-looking: her face too bony, her jaw too dominating, the whole lacking some subtle harmony that had been there before. Most people strike me as about the same "after" as "before," obviously shaped differently but neither more nor less attractive.

What *is* it that makes someone attractive, good-looking, or appealing to me? On afternoon talk shows about fat and attractiveness, the supportive voices from the audience say, "It's what's inside that counts." But that just endorses the same old dichotomies—between mind and body, between fat people (who may have "inner beauty") and beautiful appearances (which fat people do not have). I do see a beauty, manifested physically, in myself and others, just as objective as the "figure flaws" and "thunder thighs" I used to see. What is this? And when people are wonderful enough to call me beautiful—and mean it—what are they seeing?

I am not sure, but so far I have isolated two basic words: "action" and "proportion." Action is what bridges what's inside and the outside world, the mechanism by which virtues and thoughts are made real to others. Actions like donating to charity or helping a friend may be beautiful primarily in a metaphorical sense, but "action"—movement, gesture, even standing or sitting—can literally be beautiful or ugly. As such, it may sometimes be related to body size, but definitely need not be. I am tempted to become a vitalist, here. Some people seem more vivid, more *themselves*, than others. This, I think, will always be attractive, if we let ourselves see it in others and manifest it ourselves.

By "proportion" I mean something much broader than the usual sense of the word, and almost the opposite of superficial "36-24-36" measurements. To the viewer, proportion is an appreciation of the relationships among the parts of the body, and how they achieve harmony, with beauty residing in the integrated whole. I don't know why this seems easier to see in some people than others. Maybe I've just substituted other standards for the weight-based one. If so, at least the range of beauty I see is both wider and more interesting than before. And, last but not at all least, it seems (most of the time) to include me, which I can't help but think is an improvement.

The greatest aid I've had in self-acceptance is the support of others concerned with these same issues—some further down the road than I, some I could help along, but all peers in the same fight—and most of all the love (and often obviously genuine desire) of those close to me. Human beings are social animals, and what others say does matter. But we can choose the kinds of people to listen to and owe it to ourselves to do so. The right people are out there, if we look.

In my late teens or early twenties, I identified one of my major problems as "Crazy Miranda syndrome," referring to the song about a woman of that name by Jefferson Starship: "she wants all the pretty boys beside her/to write some pretty words to guide her/to tell her they love her body as well as her mind." I knew others found my mind interesting, attractive, and even lovely, but I had no such evidence about my body. I might or might not have believed the evidence if it had been offered, but the point remained moot for some time. I know that I changed, gaining self-confidence in many areas and paradoxically working toward loving myself as I am despite a roller-coaster ride of weight changes. But I also think some benevolent fortune worked with me, introducing me to people who could accept me and help me on my journey to where I want to be.

My last birthday was a turning point in some ways: especially, as I enter the second half of my threescore-and-ten years, I will shift another balance, finally having spent more time free of dieting than preoccupied with and controlled by it. I've always had an intuition (or superstition) that my life would turn wonderful when I was thirty-five. For the most part it has, although many of the best aspects are different from anything I could have imagined.

I thought that eventually, when I was down to the right weight, I could afford to eat sensibly, and my weight would remain stable. And though I never reached that weight, I now eat when (and only when) hungry, and my weight remains stable. I thought I would become thin, and then I would be "pretty," and men would like me. Though I know I'll never be thin (if I'm lucky, in this world of AIDS and cancer), I've had my share of lovers and have settled down in an enduring relationship, in which not a day goes by without me being told I'm beautiful as well as beloved. I never reached my goal weight, but I know I do have willpower: to think and feel and write and talk, to understand and to confront, to cherish and improve and accept and challenge. Not to diet, but to love and be loved and—hardest of all—to love myself as I am.

At worst, my dieting was a self-caused problem—misery, undertaken to fix myself when I wasn't broken, which itself has left some fractures and cracks. At best, it was a well-intentioned mistake—the wrong tool for the right job, which could never quite do what it promised, but did some good almost despite itself. I still have the same goals: love, self-control, beauty, success, happiness. But now I choose to seek them directly, instead of through fluctuations in my body weight.

What can I say? It works.

Underneath It All

Dixie Colvin

The dark beneath the covers was the only place I felt comfortable making love. I wouldn't assume a superior position or make love in daylight because my fat would be before my husband to see and, oh no, to reach out and caress. Large, soft breasts invite touch, which was acceptable, but stroking my belly or my "thunder thighs" wasn't.

My husband and I created an angry, devastating "intimate" relationship. I blamed his lack of desire on repression. He blamed me for being controlling. Tragically, both right, we couldn't stop the ugly accusations. I left the relationship, determined to build my self-esteem and become a sexually healthy woman.

For many years, the belief that I couldn't be sensuous *and* fat imprisoned me in flannel gowns, white bras, and full-cut cotton undies. I thought my body an eyesore to be hidden away under dark clothing. Continually hearing "What a pretty face, but . . .," I wanted to hide my body.

My journey to positive self-esteem began by searching for a transforming sexual relationship. I decided I wouldn't settle for unsatisfying affairs and I affirmed that I would have the perfect relationship. I saw other heavy women in intimate unions. But where were my loving caresses? What was wrong?

I discovered through supportive friends and books like *You Can Heal Your Life* (by Louise L. Hay) that I first needed to love myself and accept my body as it was. Every day I declared, "I love myself just the way I am. I am a beautiful woman with a healthy and perfect body." Past negative programming made it extremely difficult for me to believe what I was affirming. I wanted to attach buts—"I'm too fat," "my hair is thin," "my breasts sag," and on and on. One friend kept saying, "Fake it till you make it," so I continued the affirmations *without* the addenda.

One day, something unexpected happened. In the mirror stood a beautiful woman—ME! Physically the same, but radiance sparkled from inside. A major turning point!

I grew my hair longer and saw it as crowning my lovely body. Although it was difficult, because I still embraced the "blimp" image, I bought lacy, glamorous underclothes; long, flowing robes; and several silk teddies. With a sense of adventure, I wore them for my own pleasure, for the secret of how beautiful they were beneath my colorful new clothes—colors I had never before been brave enough to wear because I would be too visible. Dressed in a bright blue teddy and dancing by candlelight, I discovered sensuality. My body and skin seemed alive. It was like running a movie backwards and watching a shattered cup drawn back together, becoming whole again.

I walked around my home nude. One night I even cleaned house stark naked, feeling free and uninhibited. Another night I stripped, danced to rock music, and watched myself in the mirror. My stomach jiggled, and although I didn't like it, I wasn't repulsed. The curve of my hips and the set of my shoulders were a pleasure to watch.

I began indulging in fantasies—scenarios by daylight, in exciting places like beaches or mountains, in which I did risqué things entirely for the fun of it. As a next step, I wrote erotic fiction. At first I checked over my shoulder, wary of someone watching or judging my improper behavior. I discovered the only critical judge lived inside me, that terrible monster who never approved of anything I did and wanted me back in full-cut cotton.

Joy welled up from my deepest being. People commented on how beautiful I was looking. I hadn't lost an ounce of weight. Often a man would express interest as he looked directly at me—not beyond me—with a smile. With an arm lingering on my shoulder after a hug, a man might ask for my phone number. All of this I found, astonishingly, terrifying. I suddenly felt thrust on center stage, floodlights glaring on my body—a body with stretch marks, wrinkles, bulges, and cellulite. The old fear of rejection for being fat and ugly grabbed my heart and clamped tight.

Stumbling offstage, I withdrew into a cocoon of fear. Dressing conservatively again, I buried my racy underwear in my bottom drawer, suppressed my joy and laughter, stopped smiling at men, and avoided hugs. I decided any man who paid me attention suffered from some defect—"needs too much mothering," "too uptight," "too young," and so forth. I mentally annihilated all prospects.

However, feeling unworthy of positive attention wasn't comfortable anymore, either. I missed feeling joyful, laughing, and dancing. I hated expecting someone to say ugly things or to ignore me.

A friend told me, "Courage is fear that has said its prayers." I clung to this idea. "I am whole, powerful, beautiful, strong, and loving," I reaffirmed. I rescued my lacy underwear and bright clothing, bathed with perfumed soaps, and played music for dancing again. Smiling at men took extra effort, but I did it. I slowly advanced, reminding myself that growth is two steps forward, one step backward, and that I didn't have to be perfect, only courageous.

An illuminating experience happened late one afternoon when I approached a man normally very receptive to me with hugs, nice comments, and direct, appreciative eye contact. This day I received none of that, and I asked him what was wrong. He said he was tired and hungry, but I couldn't leave it there. I made a sarcastic comment about how he didn't like being around me and even called myself a bitch. I stomped away, feeling very rejected. I had, in fact, created his disapproval. Our discussion the next day further clarified his fear of intimacy and my need to feel rejected—and how our interaction had aggravated both.

A major test came when a relationship reached the sexual intimacy crossroads. A man I had been dating called, saying, "I really like you. Your mind is intriguing. I enjoy your company. But . . . I'm just not physically attracted to you." My hurt reaction sprang from my old belief that something was wrong with me. Amazingly, within hours of examining my feelings, I knew I was okay, that I was a beautiful person in spite of social prejudice. Saddened because this man had judged me by superficial criteria, I was also relieved that I knew before we had become more involved. And I was grateful for the wonderful things our relationship had given me: a connection with my passion, a clearer definition of what I was unwilling to accept, and an understanding that rejection needn't devastate me, as it once had.

"As life unfolds, there's bound to be some wrinkles" is a saying I've always remembered. I'm glad this particular set of wrinkles has been ironed out. In the process I have gained an inner strength, a knowledge of my beauty, a connection to my spirituality. And drawers emptied of boring underwear.

Pat Kite

To Food, With Peace

Pat Kite

I am tired of the tyranny of so-called overweight. Since the age of thirteen, I have tried to lose the same twenty-seven pounds. I have imbibed only water for days on end. I have ingested so many saccharides that if a similar amount were given to laboratory rats, the anti-animal experimentation leagues would protest.

I have lived for a week on lettuce, carrots, green beans, and other despised vegetables, grimacing as I swallowed, telling myself that thinness was worth it. The few times I achieved my goal, it wasn't worth it. Instead of successful, I felt frantic. After the effort to take it off came the effort to keep it off. Never peace. Self-contempt when I put the weight on again. I always did.

Is there a weight-control pill on the market that I haven't tried? The caffeine-based ones make my skin crawl, make me want to tear it off. How many of them have I taken since I was thirteen? I cannot begin to count. Interspersed with them were the "pee" pills, charmingly called diuretics, but not-so-charmingly making me run to the bathroom every half hour. When the misery of the duo became too much, I took a rest, then put my body on the scale, felt shame, and went to the pharmacy again.

A minor twenty-seven see-saw pounds; heaven knows what really obese women go through. Perhaps they are walking chemical factories that jiggle, all the while looking at "real" women, Julia, Iman, Vanna turning the media wheel. Who says "real" women? My friend David, who considers himself a connoisseur and has traveled all over the world, said he has never met a man who liked skinny women. I said he exaggerated. He said, "Okay, I dare you. Find me a man who likes to count a woman's bones."

David tends to be sarcastic about these things, but he piqued my curiosity. So I started asking. A lot of men hedged the question. They said that no, they really didn't get all that excited by an emaciated female. That isn't what I meant, I persisted. I'm talking about slim versus meat on the bone.

"How slim?" "How much meat on the bone?" Mumble, mumble. "Okay," one guy finally said, "if you don't mind my being gross." I didn't. "Well . . . I like a woman with flesh I can grab ahold of."

"Do you think I'm fat?" I asked.

His eyes lit up. "Just in the right places."

Men! I went home, took off my clothes, surveyed my body in the mirror. I had a woman's breasts, a woman's hips, a woman's thighs. It was a nice, healthy, strong, fecund body. I went on another diet. I was fat, fat, fat.

Whence come the images?

From every magazine cover, with flat-chested models, ribs showing, who if dressed in rags instead of Dior would qualify for a food handout.

From television advertisements, lithe twenty-year-olds, documented and undocumented anorexics, role models for our children.

From every movie heroine. I saw a film recently in which the star was so thin, hollow cheeks and skeletal arms, it made me uncomfortable. The critics found her performance superb, an "actress to really watch."

On all sides we are bombarded. Gymnasiums: meet the perfect mate, keep your husband, live forever. Diet clinics: count the calories in everything, group therapy, prepackaged meals, amphetamines, urine injections. Even physicians are part of the conspiracy. "Put on a little weight since last time, haven't you?"

Guilt, guilt, guilt. I've been hauling around guilt for over a quarter of a century. When was the last time I ate a really good meal without counting twenty-six calories per tablespoon of sour cream on the potato? The delicious potato. I haven't truly enjoyed a potato in forever, although I've eaten many.

And steak. Juicy, medium rare, dotted with garlic, melting in my mouth. Oh, I do love a well-aged steak, filet mignon, T-bone, even though by half-way through I flagellate myself, feeling the ugly calories mount up even as I swallow.

And chocolate. Is there anything more soul-satisfying than milk chocolate, maybe with peanuts, maybe over toffee, crunch toffee? Good chocolate, fresh chocolate, is nirvana. Sometimes I've eaten an entire bar all in one gulp so I wouldn't see it. If I didn't see it, it didn't have any calories. But not any more. There are times now when I savor a chocolate bar every day for a week. Today I even had two and enjoyed every bite. I have not a shred of guilt. I can have as many chocolate bars as I like, or steak, or even sour cream on my potatoes. It is like a miracle, a miracle that occurred because of a telephone call.

It was Monday, 11 a.m., when I picked up the receiver. "This is Hank," the person said. Hank had never called me in the twenty years he had been married to my childhood friend Irene. Hank now called to say Irene is dead. I didn't even know she had been ill.

The shock hit me after I hung up the telephone. But in the brief intermission between hearing of and absorbing the death, the thought came unbidden that "she'll never have another chocolate eclair." The thought was, as I mulled on it days after, very silly. Irene had always been elegantly slim. I don't think she even liked chocolate eclairs. I really had no way of knowing. Whatever in the world brought it to mind?

But yes, I knew. Irene worked at that slenderness, prized it. What had she done without to achieve her goals? What was I doing without for a future that might end tomorrow, end today, end the next hour? What would I regret not having done if told the reaper would soon be my companion?

Oh, there are big things, like travel. But my children, whom I don't care to leave often, compensate for these things. My children are a greater pleasure than any voyage. This perspective isn't trendy, but it's true.

And maybe, being single, I might have more love affairs. But since I seldom meet anyone I want to have them with, I can do nothing about that wish.

Ahhh . . . but yes . . . I would regret not eating more chocolate. Such a little item, but it would be a cause for regret. How strange. Maybe not so strange.

All of us deprive ourselves for "tomorrow." Maybe it's money, food, a holiday, or just a day in the sun with our feet up. But suppose "tomorrow" isn't going to come, can we do something nice right now to reward ourselves for today? Don't we deserve something in this best of all possible worlds with its ups and downs and roundabouts?

I have rid myself of the so-called tyranny of overweight that I carried around for over a quarter of a century. I am not fat. I am fine. I am fine for me.

Because I am fine for me, I can have a chocolate bar whenever I want one. I can be very particular about which ones I choose. It can't be any old chocolate bar. I am not just any old person. I am a special person and I prefer special brands. Delicious. Even better tasting without guilt.

It's amazing, really, so many months after that 11 a.m. telephone call, that my weight hasn't changed. I am eating so many foods I like to eat, only the very best, that I quite expected otherwise. But then, what difference does it make? The freedom from that burden of measurement to tyrannical unreality is a wonderful freedom indeed.

Randi Ward Mochamer

She Sure Is a Ward

Randi Ward Mochamer

"Look at this child. She sure is a Ward."
"Lawd a'mercy, girl, have you grown! You sure are a Ward."
"No doubtin' this girl is a Ward, is there, now?"

Of course I was a Ward. I knew that. It was my father's name. Everyone in his Kentucky family shared that name. They also shared his body size. More than huge. As Peter Pan called Tinker Bell when she finally dreamed for herself, "Humongous!"

I never remember being thin. Oh, twice in my life I was almost thin. The first was in eighth grade; my mother made me go to Weight Watchers. I was the only kid there. Luckily, I went with a close neighbor friend, a kind of second mother who also battled her weight. Mary rejoiced with me when I reduced to a size eleven, but unlike so many others, she still accepted me when I gained that weight back. The second time I was almost thin was my senior year in high school. I jogged and counted carbohydrates down to 165. I was accepted into the singing group *Up With People*, only to be ultimately turned down because I didn't weigh 145. I continued to try to reach that magical 140 range until I was existing on baked soy nuts, pizza, and diet coke in my freshman college dorm.

I was no happier for the few months I wore my size-eleven confirmation dress. The experience of the baked soy nuts left me with erratic periods and terrible migraines. My most recent attempt at massive weight loss, the reduction of fat in my diet to less than eight grams a day, contributed to the miscarriage of a long-awaited pregnancy.

So, finally, after almost thirty-five years of struggle, I have decided to stop struggling. I will take care of me and let me just be who I am. I am fat. My sister-in-law is thin, so thin she has trouble buying clothes. My friend is so thin she is unhealthy. I am just fat. But I am healthier today than I was throughout all my years of dieting. I have rewritten the rules of my life, and the living of those rules is a freedom like none I have ever known. Each rule is for today only, so I don't dwell on yesterday, nor do I look forward to tomorrow.

1. Today I will love me just as God created me. I will not seek to redesign who I was intended to be. I am on a path of discovering who I am. How much easier that makes self-acceptance.

2. Today I will meditate on the beauty of the world and people around me. Dieting robbed me of enjoying others. So often I thought, "If only I could be that thin," or "Doesn't he notice how fat I am?" So much pleasure was lost because I could not get out of my fatness to enjoy the moment. Today I am able to walk several miles, noticing which flowers are blooming, which children are playing, which birds are singing. I no longer worry about the number of calories I am burning, because I am free from the tyranny of dieting.

3. Today I will not diet. I will no longer submit my body to the stresses of yo-yo dieting. Lose twenty pounds, gain twenty-four. That syndrome was the story of my life, and it left my health ravaged. Much better would it have been to remain at the weight I began my first diet than to have played the yo-yo game. Much better it would have been to have eaten more than soy nuts during my early college days. Much better it would have been during my pregnancy to eat the minimum requirement of 14 grams of fat for daily amino acid balance.

4. Today I will live a healthy, well-balanced lifestyle. I like eating more fruits and vegetables. I feel better when I eat whole grains and legumes. I am more alert when I do not eat sugary, high-fat foods. These reasons are valid ones on which I can base my eating plans. Unlike dieting, these measures make sense to me. I am free from counting calories, carbos, grams, anything! Likewise, I now enjoy exercising. I like my video tapes; I like to walk. Walking gets me outside myself into the world, and I need that. I love fresh air and sunshine. I used to be afraid to be seen walking. Not anymore. I am free.

5. Today I will take care of me. For years I tried to please my mother, then I tried to please my own family. I still love them, but now I care for me first. When I do so, I am much better able to care for them. Caring for me means that I keep my hair in an attractive cut, clean and well-groomed. Caring for me means that I shop for clothes that fit me now. No more do I buy dresses a size too small, hoping to be in them next month. Next month never came. Now I buy wonderful clothes: silks and woolens, sweaters and scarves, bathing suits with pearls and sequins. Like a contented cat, I bask in wonderful stained-glass colors: purple, mauve, fuchsia. No more navy blue for me. Now I choose electric blue!

6. Today I will not be judged by others. I am tired of trying to fit into other people's molds. My first memories stem from trying to be the person my mother wanted me to be. As an adult, I can look back and realize that her intense love led to her attempts to control me. Today, I am free from that control because I choose to be, and mom and I are finally friends. Furthermore, I no longer allow myself to be judged as ugly and misshapen by a media that is into ultra-thin sexiness. I can turn off the television or turn the page of a magazine just as easily as I can stand for judgment of my body size. Today, like Oprah, I can create a different impression, create a new mold—I can be me, and that "me" can be sexy, too.

7. Today I will abstain from compulsion. Much of my obesity stemmed from compulsive overeating. Oh, I am sure that somewhere in my Ward genes, there is a little fellow that has FAT written all over him; maybe he is what makes losing weight so hard for me. But that doesn't really matter. What matters is that I no longer have to hide my fears and feelings in food. I share my thoughts, needs, desires more openly than I ever have. And by doing so, food is no longer the most important thing in my life.

8. Today I will live one day at a time. This rule and my spiritual commitment to God and my family are what sustains me. There is a power and a grace in living today for today only. It makes me less likely to take things for granted. It tends to make me more productive since tomorrow is not an issue. Most of all, living one day at a time (sometimes hours or even minutes at a time) helps me stay focused, both within myself and without. At first, it seemed dangerous, this "one day at a time" approach, dangerous because it offered me a solution, a way of changing my life. For a long time, I didn't know if I had what it took to make the change. Today, I know I do.

When I finally figured out that being a Ward meant being fat, I wanted to run and hide from the world. For many years I did just that. I didn't appear to the world to be hiding. I was a top student and class leader and earned many ribbons in 4-H and speech competitions. I was in drama, band, and choir. I was so very busy—too busy to look at me, to discover the woman inside my body. I became a teacher so I could continue to hide behind what had worked as a child.

But my life was like a frayed rope. One day it snapped, and I had nowhere to hide. The issues that had defined my childhood ran like wicked undercurrents in my adult life. I had to feel the pain of years of hidden anger and frustration. I had to confront those who had hurt me and make amends to those whom I had hurt. I had to make a decision, to live or to die. I chose life. Just for today. One day at a time. Seven years ago I came out of hiding. I began a journey of self-discovery that is never-ending, for our experiences, our loves, and our feelings define who we are and who we may become. It is a thrilling journey, even for a Ward.

DeAnn G. Semler

The Bigger the Better: Ten Reasons Why

DeAnn G. Semler

1. You can eat. Food, fast, slow, and otherwise is not anathema. You can eat when you are hungry. You can eat, without fear of retribution, three meals that contain something from each of the four food groups.

2. You become ageless. Something about roundness tends to confuse people when it comes to guessing how old you are. I *still* am asked for an ID when I buy alcohol, and I'm thirty-one. I think it's ironic that celebrities like Geraldo Rivera are going to plastic surgeons and paying to have fat injected into their cheeks and lips to get that "youthful fullness," when most of them spent a lifetime trying to diet off the pudge of their youth.

3. You are intimidating. Every guy with a "Napoleon Complex" who is five feet tall or less will be drawn to you like a lemming to the sea. There is power in size, and men know it; that's why they've been pushing the cosmetic and diet industries down our throats for so long. Women, weak from starving themselves and insecure about the slightest bulge around their abdomen, aren't likely to notice or complain when they're paid less, respected less, and abused more. Larger women aren't as afraid to "throw their weight around" and many, like me, are learning to use their size to their advantage in situations involving male (or misguided female) aggression and conflict. In the words of a self-defense instructor, "When you weigh as much as your assailant, the odds even out a bit."

4. You can be a commanding presence in any room, and on stage, you are the world around which the other actors revolve. I noticed, as an acting intern at a Renaissance Faire in Wisconsin, I could take over the stage, even outdoors, quicker than any of my "lightweight" counterparts, just by using my size for comic and dramatic effect. John Candy cannot be invisible, no matter where he is during a movie scene. Robust, red-headed Conchata Ferrel (whose career I've followed since her reign on the seventies' TV show, "Hot-L Baltimore") swiped every scene she was in while on "LA Law."

During my senior year of college, I was cast in the lead role of Sam Shepard's play "Buried Child." Hallie, though she was a much older character (I was twenty-three, she was sixty-three), was a perfect part for me because she had a larger-than-life view of herself and her role in the moral upkeep of her family. A few months later, I saw the Joseph Papp production in Chicago, and the thin, older woman who played Hallie was not as well-received as I had been. A director friend commented, "She was an afterthought in their version, a ghost. You were a tigress, an oaken beam that supported the whole structure of the play."

5. People will love you for YOU, not for the mixture of genetic characteristics that compose your outer shell. I used to think it was a coincidence that most of my friends are very thoughtful, intelligent, unprejudiced, spiritually-aware people. Unsurprisingly, when it came time to date, the men who were interested in me were fascinated by my personality, my sense of self, my sense of humor, and my personal values. I in turn found that I enjoyed the company of a man more if he was looking at me as a person first and a woman second. Although men tend to compete with one another for the best-looking date, I was fortunate to be with men who looked beyond the stereotype and were proud and excited to have me on their arm. (One reason why so many men shun larger women, according to a local bookstore owner, is the scrutiny of their peers and the resultant "ribbing" if she is not a size seven. He contends that many of his buddies actually find big women sexually attractive.) One gentleman I dated owned a Belgian chocolate factory and imported the chocolates to the U.S. He considered me a perfect companion for his evenings with other confectioners, as if my size were a testament to the quality of his chocolate!

6. You become a research whiz, an intellectual, and an encyclopedia of medical terminology in self-defense. Every large woman I know has a catalog of horror stories about trips to the doctor's office. By the time I was sixteen, I had been pumped full of cortisone since age five, had been to every quack and clinic in the U.S., and was still being subjected to steroid treatment for asthma that did not respond to anything else. (Cortisone is a steroid used for treatment of arthritis, organ transplant recipients, and severe allergies and asthma. Cortisone has severe side effects, including enormous weight gain, adrenal failure, and death.)

I had been stuck with hundreds of needles for allergy tests and made to eat odd foods, to take pills that made me hallucinate, and to inhale drugs that caused me to develop upper respiratory infections. I had been told I should (a) live in a sterile "bubble" until I outgrew my asthma, (b) leave my family and move into the Center for Respiratory Research in Denver for several years of therapy, during which time I would not be allowed visitors and would be required to do whatever the doctors told me, and (c) allow myself to be used as a guinea pig for new types of drugs being tested for asthma and take larger doses of cortisone even though the risk of my not living to be a teenager would increase dramatically.

As a child, I never went to a doctor who did not comment on my steroid-induced obesity. Many doctors tried to put me on a diet, knowing that with the hormonal effect of the cortisone, a diet would not have any long-term effect on my size.

In self-defense, and because I spent so much of my childhood in hospitals and clinics, I took nursing courses in high school and worked in the local hospital in Des Moines to better understand the men (ninety-nine percent of my doctors were men) who had such control over my body for so many years. I learned much about how the medical profession works, and I realized that when a doctor says that he is "practicing" medicine, he means it literally. Doctors *don't know* thousands of things about the human body, and like any science or craft, the only way to learn is to experiment and make mistakes. Unfortunately, many doctors take the shortest and easiest route to end the symptoms of the ailment, often ignoring the disease and its causes in the process.

Realizing that I was not going to get well with the current medical establishment, I decided to read everything I could find about asthma, allergies, and weight control. To know is to be a good patient. If you are ignorant, you will be subject to whatever prejudices and misinformation your doctor has—not a good idea. I discovered by accident that learning about human anatomy, biology, and chemistry leads to ethics questions, spiritual insights, and a better understanding of the world and all its inhabitants. I did very well on my college entrance exams in the sciences. I also grew from feeling like a human pincushion with no say so in my treatment to being a formidable opponent of the cortisone cocktail pushers who believed that suppressing my symptoms was the answer to my asthma problem. I have learned, the hard way, never to take anyone's diagnosis as the last word on a health problem. Reading and research remain a habit that has stood me in good stead throughout my life.

7. Women of the future will be big, bad, & beautiful! Trends are historically cyclical. Hence, it stands to reason that as women become more prominent in society, politics, and industry, the trend toward the pre-pubescent boy with breasts figure will once more give way to the lush and healthy forms of Renoir and Rubens, Roseanne Arnold, and *Radiance* magazine. Real women, as those of us who are "fluffy" (a word I prefer to "fat") will tell you, have hips, thighs, and a waist larger than our shoe size. Think of it as fat liberation, and our version of Woodstock draws nearer. Books like Naomi Wolf's *The Beauty Myth* are gaining ground in public opinion, making more Americans rethink their previously shallow ideas about what women "should" look like and what they "should" weigh. Richard Simmons will be seen, in the future, as a social aberration, and Nutri/System will be defined as "antiquated treatment of a superstitious society bent on unhealthy termination of natural female form; see TORTURE."

8. Fashions for large women are now more readily available. Designing fashions for women who are size fourteen and up has become a billion-dollar-a-year industry. At that rate, and with the current and delightful trend toward "over-sized" comfortable clothes that are roomy and soft, we big gals will be the Cindy Crawfords of 1999! Our clothing will be the trend-setters for the new era, and Calvin Klein will be obsessed about his runway models who can't gain enough weight to make his latest designs look good. It's always nice to be ahead of your time, isn't it?!

9. Natural selection works in our favor. Women who are marathon runners or athletes who have less than seventeen percent body fat have trouble conceiving children. Therefore, we can hypothesize that fewer children will be born to the rabid runners and high-impact aerobicists, and more children will be born to larger women who eat normal food and are not fanatic about dieting. Logically, the ultra-thin women who do manage to conceive will pass on their bulimia, anorexia, and over-trained mentality to their daughters, who will die in numbers to please their parents' and society's belief that they should be shaped like a Barbie doll.

10. It may be a cliché, but fat people really can have more fun. I may not be a jolly old elf, but I manage to play, dance, and laugh with the best of them. Many of the happy icons of our society, such as Santa Claus, are portrayed as large people. How many "skinny" holidays can you think of? The witch at Halloween may be slender, but she is certainly not seen as a happy, mentally competent person. Fairy tales are rife with eating as enjoyment images. Who can imagine summer without a watermelon or football without the "Frig" and the Goodyear blimp? Look around you: "Livin' large" is what we really call living well. As more doctors become enlightened about the dangers of dieting and more exercise programs are developed for a larger clientele, more ads and TV shows will begin to depict larger people as the "in" crowd. I've been an optimist all my life and can't wait for the changes and challenges of tomorrow. Yet, my life now is the best time I've ever had. I'm glad I'm a larger woman—anything less would be livin' small!

Mothers and Daughters:
Healing the Patterns of Generations

Diane M. Ceja

Early one Sunday morning my four-year-old daughter, Veronica, was twirling around the bedroom, displaying her vibrant, plump body. Her face radiated total confidence. As Veronica finished dressing, she matter-of-factly queried, "Mommy, I'm cute, aren't I?" I smiled and hugged her. As Veronica hugged me back, she said, "Mommy, you're cute, too!"

I felt tears rushing to my eyes. They were tears of love, but also of remembered pain. I wished that my mother had accepted me as beautiful in my entirety, including my body. In Veronica's mind, there was no question that her mommy was beautiful. In my mother's mind, I would be beautiful only if I lost weight.

For the most part, my relationship with my mother has been loving. We have shared our interests in reading, sewing, cooking, and attending plays. I have been able to talk to her about almost anything, and she has understood. But my weight has always been an area of conflict, perhaps because my mother has struggled with her own issues about body size. While I was growing up, she vacillated between not caring about her weight and needing to just lose X number of pounds. I soon realized that being chunky wasn't okay.

As I grew older, life's increasing demands and stresses pounded on my self-confidence. I started using food as a pacifier. As my weight shot up, I started to hear fat clichés and pleas from my mother: "Boys will never look at you if you're fat." "You'd look better in black." "You'd be so pretty if you'd only lose some weight." "Don't eat too much." "You don't need that ice cream." "If you would lose some weight, then you could wear clothes like your sisters wear."

My mother tried to help me lose weight. She took me to the family doctor, who prescribed a diet. She encouraged me in all my weight-loss endeavors. She even steered me into my career as a dietitian, hoping that I could change my eating habits and lose weight. At the time I did it to please her, but as I began to study I found nutrition quite interesting. Although my knowledge about nutrition increased with each degree, I continued to yo-yo in my weight.

After graduate school I moved from Minnesota to California, where there were more job opportunities for me. I enjoyed the challenge of starting a new life, but I really missed my family. Once again, I started to use food to quell my anxieties and loneliness.

This time, however, I fought back before my binging got totally out of control. I joined the local health club, which had weight-lifting machines and aerobic classes. I also worked on eating more nutritious foods and cutting down on sweets. Gradually I felt less stressed out, had more energy, toned up my body, lost some weight, and improved my eating habits. I felt healthier than I had for a long time.

Despite that, I still didn't have much self-confidence about my large body. Then I met Ignacio. Ignacio admired my round plumpness and viewed me as sexy and desirable. He helped me feel good about my body because he accepted and loved me as I was. When I felt depressed, sometimes I'd talk about diets and losing weight. He would tell me that I was fine just as I was. Other times, he would try to tease me out of my mood by calling me his *gordita* (little fat one) or another silly name. He attempted to make me feel better, but ultimately, I needed to accept myself.

A few years after Ignacio and I were married, I became pregnant and our daughter, Veronica, was born. She came screaming and kicking into this world with a beautiful, plump nine-pound, six-ounce body. Throughout infancy, Veronica was larger and plumper than most babies. I didn't worry about her body size until she became a toddler. Then the specter of my old issues about fatness started to darken our mother-daughter relationship.

By the age of two, Veronica was a round-faced, plump Campbell kid. She was the mirror image of me at that age, which created a sense of déjà vu when I looked at her.

Around that time I read a research paper on the development of obesity in children. The paper said there was a strong relationship between the weights of mothers and daughters. If the mother was large, the child was more likely to be large. Another finding was that fat preschool children were at risk of becoming fat teenagers. I started to worry about Veronica's future. Would it be similar to my life? The ugly clothes, the rejections, and the people who hurt me more than helped? To my horror, I caught myself admonishing her with my mother's words.

I blamed myself for Veronica's plumpness because I was plump. I thought that if I had control of my weight, then Veronica would be slim. A few months later, while visiting my parents in Minnesota, the crowning blow fell. My mother and I were discussing my weight loss, and she said, "I always wondered how you could be credible as a dietitian when you were so fat." I felt devastated. I didn't confront her or stand up for myself. I just felt awful.

I went back home with my mother's words ringing in my ears. I spent a lot of time thinking about how my weight was still controlling my sense of self-esteem. I didn't want to poison Veronica's positive view of her body and herself. I especially didn't want Veronica to waste time having self-doubts and continually dieting or thinking that she needed to. Finally, I didn't want to continue depending on my mother's or other people's opinions to validate my own sense of self-worth.

I tried to figure out how to deal with my insecurities and to nurture my relationship with Veronica. I realized that first I needed to pay more attention to myself. I had to clean up my own excess baggage (past memories and fears) and work on accepting myself as I was. I read everything that I could on developing a positive self-image. I didn't lose weight. Instead, I took every opportunity to nurture and feel good about me. I went for long walks and did special things for myself: I got facials and haircuts, bought clothes, and spent many quiet moments by myself.

I also worked to stretch my inner self. I actively pursued jobs and projects that interested me and explored new opportunities. As a dietitian, I have taught classes, published a newsletter, worked in research, written articles, and counseled clients. One of my most enjoyable experiences was teaching classes for a nearby health club. I loved teaching there because I was able to stress self-acceptance and making healthy food choices. As a large woman, I projected an exuberant, healthy image, and my students and I had a wonderful time. Right now I divide my time between my family, volunteer work as a nutrition consultant at a Head Start program, and writing.

Veronica is now four years old, and I have tried to build a strong relationship with her. I focus on loving her for who she is, and I encourage her to explore new interests and new possibilities.

I have set certain goals for myself in relation to her. I don't expect to always succeed, but I am going to do my best. Here are some of the goals:

1. To give Veronica a strong sense of herself. To help her identify and develop her strengths and learn to be patient with herself as she practices what is difficult for her. To give her some space so that she can explore on her own.

A few weeks ago our family went to the park. Veronica was fearlessly climbing jungle gyms and swooshing down steep slides. She zoomed down a twelve-foot slide and landed hard on her rear. Ignacio said, "Are you okay?" After determining that she was fine, he said, "You really came off that slide fast. Good thing that you have a little extra padding back there." Veronica giggled, and then triumphantly marched over to the spiral slide and climbed up again. Ignacio's example continues to encourage me in my parenting goals.

2. To help her feel emotionally strong. Crying and other expressions of all feelings are allowed and encouraged.

3. To help Veronica develop tenacity. I would like her to always try, even if others say she won't be able to do something. After a good try, however, she can reassess the situation, pat herself on the back for trying, and then move forward or go in another direction. My tenacity has helped me to achieve many things that I value in life, and I want to pass this on to her.

4. To teach her that a person who is plump does not need to deny herself, nor does she need to feel unworthy in any way. I encourage her, instead, to live life to its fullest and to shoot for the sky in her dreams.

5. To expose Veronica to a wide variety of activities—in sports, literature, music, and other areas. Ignacio and I have very different tastes in music, so Veronica is exposed to many different styles, including ranchera and salsa.

We all love baseball, so when possible, we participate in or watch games. I'm encouraging Ignacio to teach Veronica how to play his favorite sport, soccer. I think that she definitely displays the spunk and instincts to be a good player. Veronica and I do a lot of walking, an activity we have both enjoyed since she was very young.

6. To assist her in putting food in its proper perspective. Food should nourish the body and please the palate. Veronica and I are working on being more open to trying new foods. Often she will come home from preschool and will amaze me by telling me what new food she tried that day. Her ending statement is usually, "And Mommy, it was really good!"

7. Finally, to learn from Veronica about how to be a mother who helps her daughter feel good about herself—a mother who supports rather than obstructs, who encourages rather than limits, and who loves her child for who she is rather than what I or others would like her to be.

As I go into the living room for a short writing break, I glance at Veronica, who is mimicking the gyrating movements of a dance troupe on TV. She stops gyrating to inquire, "Mommy, I really dance good, huh?" I reply, "Yes, Veronica, you really do!"

As for my relationship with my mother, it is still loving. I have always admired my mother's independence and emotional strength, and I hope to pass those qualities on to Veronica. But we haven't totally resolved our differences about weight. In some ways, we're like two boxers tensely circling each other before the start of a match. We're both waiting to see who will be the first to shake hands.

I did detect a slight softening in my mother's attitude when we last spoke long distance. I told her about *Radiance* magazine and how the articles promoted a positive self-image and discussed the accomplishments of large women. She surprised me by saying it sounded great. She also commented that she knew many successful people who were large. I replied that being large didn't affect your knowledge or your competence, even in health-related occupations. She agreed and mentioned a large nurse who was competent and had a wonderful rapport with her clients and their families.

After I hung up the phone, I found myself wishing that we could have settled our conflicts about weight once and for all. Unfortunately, a problem that spans more than thirty years can't often be taken care of in one conversation.

I still intend to have a long talk with my mom about weight, my career as a dietitian, and our past weight conflicts. I want to resolve those issues so that we can enjoy and nurture our relationship. Perhaps sharing this article with her will be a step in the right direction.

Gail Picado

Fat Women Speak

Gail Picado

On the day I was born, my father reportedly said, "Show me a fat baby, and I'll show you a fat kid. Show me a fat kid, and I'll show you a fat adult."

With those words, it seems my destiny was set.

By the time I was in the first grade, I was a head taller and twenty pounds heavier than all the other children my age. I was the first to reach 100 pounds by the fourth grade, and I experienced my first liquid starvation diet on entering the seventh grade. I felt real proud to have squeezed into a size fourteen. I didn't care that others were wearing a size seven. All that mattered was that in junior high school, I would not have to suffer the humiliation of being weighed by the school nurse in front of my classmates, as was the ritual in elementary school.

My parents were uncomfortable with my large size. Dad was very verbal about it, but my mom tried to help by sewing clothes with straight lines only. No pleats or ruffles for me, only straight lines to give a slimmer look. I wanted ruffles and pleats.

At some point, my father convinced himself (and me) that I should have been born a boy instead of a girl, purely based on my size. As luck would have it, my younger brother was a runt, so I continually heard my father say, "If only Steve would grow as big as Gail, we'd have a quarterback for the football team."

Reinforcing my father's statement that I should have been born a boy, I had to deal with the insecurity of being a late bloomer in puberty. All my friends had their periods by the age of thirteen, so on my sixteenth birthday, when I still did not have my period, I knew for certain that God had made some kind of terrible mistake and that I really should have been a boy. I had read about people being born the wrong sex. My dad had repeated his comment that I should have been a boy so many times that I lay awake many nights worrying about God's judgment. But time proved my dad wrong, and I soon found that I really had only one problem: my weight.

At the start of tenth grade, I weighed twenty pounds more than my father, so it was no surprise when he decided that I would never be asked out on a date. To remedy that problem, dad bought me a car. He didn't want me to have to sit home while other girls went out on dates. But boys did ask me out, and each time I could see the look of bewilderment on my dad's face. He probably wondered, but was afraid to ask, if I was giving away sexual favors to get dates. I wasn't.

Now that I am forty-three years old, and every diet known to man is behind me, I've grown to accept my larger size. It's kind of sad to say that others have not. My current boss is a good example. She is 5'7" and weighs 110 pounds. She never allows herself to eat more than fifteen grams of fat a day. From the first day she was hired as the Chief Financial Officer, she judged me unsuitable for my position as Personnel Manager. It didn't matter that I had already been doing the job successfully for five years. In her opinion, anyone who could not control her weight could not handle any position higher than paper-clip sorter. With that opinion, she set out on her personal attempt to make me miserable enough to quit.

Lucky for me, my boss didn't understand my personality. The more she tried to dump on me and force me out, the more determined I was to show her how wrong she was to judge me incompetent because of my large size. After a year and a half of meeting every challenge she threw my way, I realized the only way I would win her over was to ask her about her low-fat diet and to try to lose some weight myself. I tried to acquire a disgust for fat. I really tried. Really! I even lost seventeen pounds. But then life got boring. Food tasted like cardboard. So I added a few extra grams of fat to my diet and gained back seven pounds.

My boss used to tell me how embarrassed she was years ago when she weighed 145 pounds. (I should be so lucky.) She just HAD to do something about it because she was "just so fat!" Now, she complains about her fingernails breaking and her hair falling out in clumps. I just smile to myself because I haven't told her about the article I read that said women who lose weight by cutting fat from their diet experience nail breakage and hair loss. I wonder if she'll be as embarrassed about having a bald head as she was about being "SO FAT!" I don't plan to tell her about the article. It's her punishment for being thin.

I do enjoy shocking thin, single women I meet with the number of marriage proposals I've had: twenty-seven. My first marriage lasted seven years. I know now that it was doomed from the start. Anyone who has ever fought the numbers on a scale should never marry a man who falls in love with a seventeen-year-old girl only because she has long, blonde hair. But then, I felt lucky. After all, this was my first marriage proposal and I had to be lucky because my father had convinced me that I should be buying my dresses from "Omar the tent-maker." I thought at the time that I probably would not get a second chance. Little did my father or I know!

My second marriage only lasted five months. I got talked into marriage by a man who needed an instant family for his tax return. But my third marriage of eleven years has been great. I have a husband who finds me very pleasing to the eye. Love truly is in the eye of the beholder.

I always look back in humor at my encounters with the Department of Motor Vehicles, with all the name changes required with each marriage. When I changed my name on my driver's license after my third marriage, the clerk at the D.M.V. said in a grumpy tone, "I hope you found one you like this time. I can't even get one man, and you've had three."

At first I didn't understand men's attraction to me. After all, I grew up being told that I would have no one unless I became thin. How I wish I had the wisdom then that experience and age have given me. Look around, most singles are thin. They practically kill themselves every night in the exercise gyms and don't have a clue to the secret of finding a good mate.

A man doesn't fall in love with a thin woman only because she's thin. Oh, he'll look and give it some thought, but what he really looks for in a life-long relationship with a woman is sweetness. Yes, sweetness. That's the secret. Men call it sexy, but it's really sweetness.

Think about it. My experience has been that most thin women complain more and demand more than large women because they think they look good and are confident they can replace their men with better ones at the drop of a hat. But a large woman is more apt to soothe and comfort a man in hard times because she knows that he has faults just like she has.

Sexy isn't thin. Sexy is cleanliness with a tasteful appearance added to sweetness. Every man who has ever asked me to marry him has named that one quality, sweetness, as a reason he was in love with me. I would counter by asking, "But, doesn't me being fat bother you?" (That's my insecurity speaking out. Remember, I was raised being told I had to be thin for a man to love me.)

Their response was always the same. "You're so sweet. I can't get enough of your sweetness."

But I like my husband's answer the best. He nuzzles up to me and says, "You're like a Cadillac. You're built for comfort . . . and you're awfully sweet, too."

Debbie Bowling

Heavy Interviews

Debbie Bowling

In my late twenties, I moved to a new state to be near my family. My Master's degree and four years of experience working with troubled youth afforded me the confidence to leave my job. Within a few weeks of moving I had my first interview at a psychiatric hospital for adolescents. Ten minutes after the scheduled appointment time, a short, thin man emerged from his office. His hand briefly touched his beard as he introduced himself and motioned me toward a chair. After seating himself, he picked up my resume and waved it at me.

"You have impressive credentials." He reached over and put the resume close to the edge of the desk near me, then stared into my face. "However, after seeing you today, I probably would not hire you because of your weight." He leaned back suddenly in his chair. "Have you considered therapy for your weight problem?" I nodded, and he continued, "In this facility, public relations with parents are important. We are a treatment facility and do not want anyone working here who gives the impression that they have an emotional problem. In fact, many children are brought here by their parents because they are too fat and cause their parents embarrassment and concern."

Numbly I got up and walked out of the office and drove home. For many interviews following this experience I found myself withdrawing, becoming unable to present myself or my ideas. I held an image of myself as a person who was too big—too big to have meaningful ideas or contributions. Certainly, too big to demand that I be considered for a job for which I was qualified.

After several months, I found it more and more difficult to go to job interviews. I no longer allowed my normally outgoing personality to present ideas. I became quiet and withdrawn, hopeful that the interviewer would not notice me or my body size. It was no surprise that I did not get a job offer during this time.

One day I decided that I should try once again to "do" something about my weight. Usually, reading a few "before and after" ads would be enough to ignite a flame within me to give yet another diet company my money, my time, and my body, but not this time. This time I decided to do it right. No fads. No weird diets. This time I would do the proper research to find out exactly how I should go about making this change permanent. The library had numerous books about weight, diet, and fat people. A few books were specifically about women. I dug into the material, searching for answers to my questions. Do fat people have emotional problems? If it is truly a matter of willpower to lose weight, how does one sustain that will-power for a lifetime?

The more I read, the more I realized the literature contained conflicting information regarding weight loss, weight gain, and weight control. The reports ranged from discussions of fat people's needs for more food to discussions that fat people do not eat much more than thin people. There were many diets and weight-reducing programs, a theory about fat cells being bigger than thin cells, a setpoint theory, and a theory that diets create a famine for the body and lower the metabolism.

What became increasingly clear, from both the literature and my experiences, was that many people lose weight and 90 percent of these same people gain it back. Permanent weight loss is so rare that no one could boast of having found a "cure" for obesity. Despite this fact, most health care providers continue to push ineffective "treatments" for fat people, namely restrictive diets. Some research suggests that these diets create a yo-yo pattern of weight loss and gain, which puts more stress on the body than the original excess weight.

A few books and articles caught my attention because of their "attitude," and I read them with care. Some material noted that the pressure to lose weight is aimed primarily at women and that unless men are significantly overweight, they continue to be socially mobile. Susan and Orland Wooley reported in *Women and Psychotherapy* (1980) that data collected in a midtown Manhattan study suggested that women declined on a social mobility scale in relation to their weight, whereas men did not. This finding was seen as further indication that women are still judged primarily on physical appearance.

Marcia Millman in *Such a Pretty Face* (1980) noted that society has progressively regarded fleshiness as unsexy and as an indication of economic worth. "... being thin is a kind of inconspicuous consumption that distinguishes the rich at a time when poor people can more afford to be fat than thin ... a woman increases her market value by being slender. Fat women are afforded a non-sexual status or granted a degraded 'lower class' kind of animal sexuality." (p. 106)

Many of the large women Millman interviewed were aware not only of their status, but also of the lower social class afforded men who preferred heavy women. Men who enjoyed friendships or sexual relations with heavy women frequently did not want to be seen in public with them.

Irene Frieze in *Women and Social Roles* (1978) discussed body size and shape as an indication of potential dominance over others. Thus, in a more brute physical sense, height, weight, and strength typically define who will be the survivor or the dominant individual in a conflict. Frieze also noted that physical size may be a nonverbal dominance message for humans (as well as for animals). No specific data exist on the effects of height for women, but most women "look up" to men, thereby reinforcing "higher" masculine status. In the same sense, extra weight may imply a "larger" and therefore more physically dominating status. In theory, the heavy woman would be more difficult to dominate than the smaller woman.

Millman adds to this view by noting that fat women are usually shown as domineering in the media and popular jokes. "Overweight women are suspected of feeding and taking care of themselves, giving pleasure to their own bodies, rather than stimulating, pleasing, and nurturing others . . . "

My search to find the correct way to lose weight left me with a dilemma. I could continue to go on diet after diet or I could modify my view of myself and other fat people. This dilemma continued to flip-flop in my mind for several years, demanding attention whenever the media highlighted a celebrity's weight loss or new diet. But for the most part, the dilemma made me angry that fat prejudice is not only real but is moreover encouraged.

As a society we have always been uncomfortable with people who are different, who do not fit some mainstream idealized "normal" person. Consequently, African-Americans are expected to try to become white, homosexuals to become straight, Jews to become Christians, and fat people to become thin people. It is part of this expectation to change what cannot be changed that creates classes of people who either fight for acceptance or focus energy on what they cannot accomplish.

Intolerance creates messages of shame and non-acceptance that do not value the person or the unique gifts and talents of the person. A lack of self-acceptance can rob a person of her spirit and allow her talent and gifts to be buried under self-doubt and insecurity. This was happening to me, and after some soul-searching I decided that I would not allow myself to wait until I was "thin enough" to go after what I knew I wanted, including a job. Since I was large, I must accept it, recognize the positives of it, and convey my positive attitude to others including interviewers. Like all people who deal with discrimination, I had to work to bolster my self-esteem against stereotypes and negative humor, and, of course, I had to be better qualified than the average applicant. Most of all, I had to accept that some people will never change their attitudes, but many people will.

My next interview was with a board of directors. I prepared myself with meditations and positive statements about my life and my body. I wrote out my ideas, dressed very well, made one of my best presentations, and eventually I was offered the job. While the job search was victorious, it was only one change in my life and my thinking, and I later encountered other people who expressed their negative attitudes about fat people.

While developing a personal philosophy and attitude is important, it is also critical to be part of a supportive network. A network not only provides connections with other people who will listen to you and nurture you, but it also allows you to express your anger about discrimination to others and work together with them to make changes in the world.

Celebrating the Outlaw Within,
or "Ride'em Fatgirl"

Debra Derr

It does stretch the imagination. Too nervous to steal and loath to commit any act of violence beyond scolding my cat, I admit I'm hardly the image of the essential outlaw—but my heart will tell you differently.

My heart can hear the ring of spurs as I walk through the dusty streets. I have twin pearl-handled six shooters strapped to my full thighs and a deck of marked cards in my vest pocket. My heart sees the Wanted poster with my name on it hanging in the Wells Fargo office, although my heart thinks my cheeks are drawn way too puffy. My horse Paint runs like the wind and my heart knows Paint can outrace any posse, as long as I lean forward in the saddle and keep my weight off her kidneys so she doesn't have to stop and pee all the time.

I'd like to flaunt my maturity and say that this is just a childhood fantasy, born of "Gunsmoke" reruns and the memory of my Dale Evans cowgirl outfit (chubbette). I'd like to say that, but I'd be lying. My outlaw persona evolved along with a growing sense of self-love, learned as I entered my thirties. What took so long? One reason may be the lack of suitable role models.

The boys in the neighborhood had Billy the Kid, Jesse James, and Butch and Sundance to emulate. They practiced shooting each other in the back and dealing from the bottom of the deck, skills that would stand them in good stead later in life when they got to law school. As a mere girl, I fretted on the sidelines and wondered why there were no great women outlaws.

In college, I learned there were a few. Belle Starr is the one most people remember, possibly because the only clear photograph of her reveals a woman who had a face that could stop a clock. The general opinion of Belle's sociopathy was that she needed to compensate for her ugliness by punishing society with her crimes.

Then there was Etta Place, the pretty schoolmarm who rode with the Hole in the Wall Gang and helped Butch Cassidy and the Sundance Kid pull off a string of bank robberies. The consensus on Etta was that she was clearly a nymphomaniac and cross-dresser. Nowadays that lifestyle would earn her a spot on the Donahue show, but back then, it didn't satisfy my longing for a heroine/heavy.

As a fat child (and even later as a fat adult) I have always felt some degree of alienation from those around me. Although I was sociable and liked people, I liked my solitude, too, and spent many happy hours alone. This solitude led to the development of a rich inner life. Part fantasy, part philosophy, fed by a voracious reading habit, my inner life was always rewarding. Growth and change were welcome, natural features of this life.

In the real world, life was different. Painfully I discovered that growth and change were looked on with suspicion. I realized that certain things were expected of me as a fat woman. People seemed to need to see me as a stereotype, not as an individual. This need manifested itself in the oddest ways. When I wanted to wear clothing other than the bullet-proof polyester usually reserved for fat women, I was told, "But this is what you like." When I went to a riding stable other than the one where I'd taken lessons for years, I was pegged as a tyro and given an aged, docile mare to ride because "She'll suit you." When I aced a difficult psychology exam in college, the professor said, "I didn't think you were this bright."

It took a while, but I began to realize that these people were angry with me! I'd had the audacity to rock their images of what a fat person should be—sloppy, incompetent, stupid—and these people hated it. They needed to feel superior, which required an inferior with whom to compare themselves. Sometimes they would choose a person of African descent for this role, or a Jew, or a gay person. In this case, they chose a fat person.

There are two likely responses to bigotry: get mad or get even. Mad is a powerful motivator. Legitimate anger at injustice was, after all, one reason many of our ancestors fled to North America. Turned inward, however, that righteous wrath becomes an unhealthy force and leads to severe depression and even physical illness. Getting even is a way of dealing with anger. The difficult part about getting even is finding a socially acceptable way of doing so. Devoting oneself to a life of crime may seem tempting at first, but it's tough to get credit. There hasn't been a Robin Hood since the Middle Ages, but there have been plenty of Ted Bundys.

Finding a constructive response to years of negative imaging seemed impossible, but in the end I found the life I had been living inside myself was the life that now belonged in the daylight. I became an outlaw. That may sound pretty funny coming from someone who has never committed a crime and seems hell-bent each year on overpaying her taxes. Okay, so I'm no Etta Place.

But I have an anger inside, a rebelliousness that has changed me from a natural victim into a self-made victor. It finally became clear that my longing for an outlaw role model was my need for an example of someone who was, for better or worse, respected. My child's instincts favored those who, though shunned by the society in which they lived, were admired (albeit grudgingly) for their individuality.

Criminality alone doesn't make an outlaw. What makes an outlaw is the cavalier disregard of others' expectations. What makes an outlaw is a steadfast refusal to live within the narrow confines of society. (Perhaps criminality is the unimaginative, immature response to those confines.) Most of all, what makes an outlaw is his or her willingness to be different.

Once I acknowledged the outlaw in myself—a fat woman with self-regard—I started to notice other outlaws around me: Women who worked in non-traditional jobs, artists, bikers, the kid in the Nirvana t-shirt with a passion for Tolstoy. All of us have this basic contradiction within ourselves, and something more: a secret joy, an inner life to see us through.

Every time I demand respect, every time I insist on my basic rights, I celebrate the outlaw within me. Watching the shock register on the face of some bully who thought he could demean the fatgirl thrills me to the marrow. Refusing to be stereotyped as worthless validates my own innate sense of self-worth. My inner outlaw is vindicated whenever I won't live down to someone else's expectations of me.

Perhaps when we, as a culture, become tolerant of each other's differences the need for an outlaw class will dissolve, which may be for the best. But some of us may not be too sure; I would hate to surrender the outlaw in me. I don't think I could. After all, it's something to be the biggest, baddest, toughest taxpayer west of the Hackensack River.

Patt Jackson

A Vehicle for the Soul

Patt Jackson

Though I've been fat all my life, self-acceptance has not come naturally. I struggled with it for years and still occasionally have to work at it.

I was a chubby baby who became a fat child. I had unfortunately been christened with the name Patti, which meant other kids didn't even have to stretch their imaginations to come up with rhyming insults. Not only was I fat, I was also tall—an Amazon among my peers. No one let me know it was okay to be large or encouraged me to concentrate on the things I did well, so I believed all the negative remarks I heard around me.

Fat became my identity. I believed that was all I was: fat, freakish, unlovable, unloved. My grade school years were just a small preview of the horror I would face in my teen years. While other kids were excelling in academics, sports, and dating, I was barely passing my classes and spent agonizing hours devising ways to get out of swim and gym classes. The highlight of my day came at 3:30, when I could escape to my room and hide from the world. My self-esteem was nonexistent.

When I was eighteen, I married the first man I dated. He was twenty-six and in the Army, and I saw this marriage as my ticket to independence and acceptance. My husband was the first person who ever told me he loved me, but since I was filled with such self-loathing I assumed something had to be horribly wrong with him. The marriage lasted only nine years, but it was an important first step on my long road to self-acceptance.

After my divorce, I joined a diet club and lost seventy-five pounds. Was my life better? I can't say. For the first time I lived on my own, in a city hundreds of miles from my family. I worked three jobs and was too busy to notice the tremendous changes I was undergoing. Another major first was happening in my life: I started to meet men at work and date them. Something my friends started in their junior high school years, I was just discovering at age twenty-seven.

Though I'd lost weight, I was still fat. But suddenly I was meeting men who found me funny and smart and attractive just the way I was. It was an amazing time in my life. I began to see that I was things other than just fat; I was someone who had a nice personality, who was clever and energetic and resourceful, and who could make good friends of both sexes. I began to discover things about myself that had nothing to do with my weight. I began to see the person inside me. I was another few miles down that road to self-acceptance, and finally I was enjoying the journey.

I moved back to my home town, got an apartment, a new job, and a new life, and gained back the seventy-five pounds plus a few more. I began to pay closer attention to people I met. Some were intelligent and funny, some were not so bright. Some were gentle and loving, some were rude and obnoxious. Some were happy in good relationships, some were struggling with bad ones. I saw that none of these things seemed related to people's appearances and body sizes, and I realized that good things happened to fat people, just as miserable things happened to thin ones.

I thought a lot about this revelation. I wondered why I had always chosen to define myself as fat, rather than any other way. Eventually I came across the comment that a body is merely a vehicle for a soul, and this simple idea seemed to crystallize my thoughts. I realized that who you were came from things inside you, your thoughts and actions and hopes. Your body was just the vehicle that carried everything around. And like any other vehicle, the body could be fixed up or left to rust; it could be compact or mid-sized or even a luxury model. It wasn't so much what you had as what you did with it. I'd passed another milestone.

About this time, I became acquainted with a fat acceptance group: men and women who were fat and apparently content with the status quo, and the men and women attracted to these people. I went to a convention expecting to find assorted freaks and oddballs, but what I actually found was a group of very caring, compassionate, and understanding people who also knew how to throw a good party. For the first time in my life I felt like part of a group, rather than a solitary blob on the sidelines. I also discovered what it felt like to be the homecoming queen and belle of the ball all in one night! I was still fat, still insecure, but suddenly I felt beautiful and desired. I've never let go of that marvelous feeling.

Today when I ask myself how my life would be different if I were 100 pounds lighter, I find I have no answer. I've been married and divorced, and I've been in several love relationships, good and bad. I've traveled a great deal, I enjoy good health, and I have a loving family and many good friends. I had a long career in one field and am now starting my own small business and pursuing new interests. What more could being thin possibly add to my life? And how much of my life did I waste in the useless pursuit of wishing to be thin?

Being fat has taught me things. Discriminated against as a child, I learned to be more compassionate and sensitive to others. I learned how easy it is to make someone feel loved, and I know from experience how easy it is to bruise a human spirit. The journey to self-acceptance has also taught me these lessons: Be the best person you can be. Concentrate on the things you're good at and enjoy this brief, exciting time on earth. Expend your energy on the things that really matter and know that your body size is not one of them.

Your self-esteem is not measured by a number on a scale; it's measured by your deeds. You may travel through life as a luxury sedan on a highway of compacts, but don't ever lose sight of your precious cargo.

Jane Dwinell

Homesteading: Building a House, Housing a Spirit

Jane Dwinell

It's Monday morning. I rise when I've had enough sleep, no jangling alarm clock at my side. The rest of the family—Sky, my partner; Dana, my four-and-a-half-year-old daughter; and Sayer, my one-year-old son—may or may not be up. Like me, they rise with their natural rhythms. We start our day. There are animals and people to feed. There is work to be done. But no one showers, primps, dresses, and hops in a car. We work at home.

Depending on the season, there may be gardens to tend, food to harvest and preserve, trees to cut and pull out of the woods, wood to split and stack. Perhaps chickens need to be slaughtered, a playhouse built, the lawn mowed, a thousand gallons of sap boiled down into maple syrup. As the day goes on, I may sit down at the computer to write, Sky may speak to some clients on the phone or leave for a couple of hours for a meeting or mediation session. We may decide it's time to play and head for the beach or the slopes or to load the canoe onto the car for some river running.

In the middle of all this activity, two children tag along. Dana helps pick raspberries or stack wood. Sayer rides in the backpack for the best view. Periodically they get parental time, for reading, computer play, nursing, or some pushes on the swing. We move in time to the seasons and the individual. If one parent needs some time off or a nap, he or she takes it. If we are hungry, we eat. We have no schedules here, no structure other than the copious lists that may or may not be needed. We do what needs to be done.

We are homesteaders. We earn our way by doing as much as we can for ourselves, and when we need cash we sell our maple syrup, salsa, eggs, and vegetables. When Sky and I need contact with the "outside world" (and a little more money), he mediates with families in conflict and I write about my life and experiences. It is a peaceful, happy life, one I would not trade for anything.

My life has not always been this joyful. From the time I was small, my life was filled with conflict, anger, and frustration about three things: my body, my sexuality, and my deep desire to change the world.

I have always been chubby. As a small girl I was embarrassed by clothes that did not fit and jokes from my brothers. As a teenager I blamed my lack of popularity on my body but never seriously dieted. As a young woman I moved from fad diet to fad diet, embracing everything from vegetarianism to Weight Watchers. Nothing changed. There was no miracle. Whatever size I was, from 10 to 22, my life still felt empty and meaningless. I thought a thin body would guarantee happiness, great sex, and an important career. I was wrong.

I have always been sexually attracted to both men and women. In junior high and high school I ignored crushes on girls and women and longed for some boy who was clearly out of my reach. In college I was considered "fast" in my rush to find out what sex was all about. In my late twenties I swore off men altogether. In my search for the perfect partner—one who would respect me for who I was, maintain a no-sex-role household, and make love with me skillfully and gently—I was constantly disappointed.

Although my career desires have been ever-changing, I knew I wanted to do something that would have a great impact on the world. First I was going to discover a cure for cancer. When someone told me girls couldn't do that, I moved on to acting. I would be famous, but I didn't want to live in New York City or California. I decided to be a novelist, and then a historian, and then a midwife. I would deliver babies in the most family-centered fashion. But I also wanted to homestead and live a simple country life. I went to nursing school, moved to the country, and became the head nurse of Vermont's first in-hospital birthing center. For five years it seemed almost perfect—I was changing the world. I was making a difference in the lives of thousands of childbearing women, and I was living in the country, trying to develop my little homestead.

So why did I leave work every day exhausted and angry? My evening ritual hardly varied. I napped and then I ate and ate and ate. I had no energy for my garden or my animals. The firewood remained unsplit and unstacked, and I turned up the thermostat. Something was wrong. I loved being with birthing women, but it was pulling me down. I blamed my lack of energy, my lack of a partner, my unstacked wood, my dying chickens, my anger, all on my body. I was fat—that was why nothing was going right. Everything would be perfect if I were thin. Then I could really change the world.

At some point it became clear that I was not going to get thin. It also became clear that I needed to leave my job and give up my homesteading dream. I moved on to my next change-the-world fantasy—a vegetarian natural foods restaurant. Without any food service experience, I plunked down my life savings (and that of a few trusting friends) and bought a run-down café. I hired only women and bought my supplies from local organic farmers and natural food suppliers.

The Corner Café blossomed but never flourished. Because it was in a small Vermont town, there were never enough people to support the café, but those who did loved it. Various causes and candidates held meetings and fundraisers. The food was great and the staff was happy. I was busier than I had ever been in my life and much more at peace. I no longer compulsively ate, even with all that food around me, and I no longer worried about my body size. I had a string of girlfriends, but no one was right. My only source of anxiety was the amount of money I was losing every month. My next fantasy was to break even and eventually sell the café and use the money (if any) to move to a women's community in the country where I could fulfill my homesteading dream.

But I fell in love and everything changed. Sky was my Thursday afternoon produce person, delivering fruits and vegetables from the Boston market. Something clicked and I was petrified. But there was no mistaking the feeling, even though he was a man. Luckily it was mutual and our love affair began.

To make a long story shorter, I did eventually sell the café after we spent a year commuting two hours each way to see each other. I moved with Sky to a small cabin that we built ourselves, deep in the woods of northern Vermont. After a couple of months we decided to have a baby, and I became pregnant with Dana. We searched for land on which to build a homestead—his dream as well as mine—and bought this place known as Full Moon Farm. In the past five years we have built a barn, a house, and a sugar house. We have installed solar panels and other equipment to produce our own power. We have planted an orchard and vegetable, herb, and fruit gardens. We have had two children, Dana and Sayer. We have gradually become more self-sufficient.

My homesteading dream is now a reality, and I realize that I am changing the world the best way I know how—by living a self-reliant, environmentally responsible life; by sharing my feelings and experiences of that life with others through my writing and through my example; and by raising my children to be responsible, humane adults.

After years of inner questioning, I have finally accepted myself as a bisexual. I have also learned that the important thing about sex is not the label but the love.

As for my body and my quest for thinness? My body size no longer makes a difference to me. What is important is my strength and my health. Homesteading is hard physical work, the hardest I have ever done. Pregnancy, childbirth, nursing, and parenting are also demanding physical work. At some point, my body "goal" moved from being thin to being strong, fit, and healthy. I built this house with my brain as well as my coordination and strength. I carried heavy timber, I lifted walls into place, I installed windows and plasterboard. And every time I whined or complained, Sky reminded me gently but firmly that I was as strong as he was.

I also want my children to be accepting of different body sizes and to learn to eat only when they are hungry, to learn to trust the inner wisdom of their bodies. I want to show them that it is all right to have feelings of anger or of happiness, and that they can express those feelings and their family will still love them. I want to show them that— miraculously—they don't have to eat those feelings. I have discovered that the best way to teach my children is for me to practice what I preach. Gradually, patiently, I have accepted my body and everyone else's for the size and strength and beauty that each holds.

The other day I was picking wild blackberries with my family along an old, muddy dirt road. Dana and I walked through a giant puddle and I slipped and fell, hard. After reassuring myself that I hadn't spilled any berries out of my pail and that I was just a little wetter than before, Dana and I laughed about my fall. Then she looked up at me and said, "You fell that hard because you are so heavy and strong." Ten years ago I would have been broken up inside by what I would have perceived as an insult. But that day, seeing the love-light shine in my daughter's eyes and smile, I realized she was giving me her highest compliment.

So here I am, heavy and strong, proud of what this body has done for me—built my home, raised my food, made love with my best friend, birthed my babies, and housed my spirit. And I love her with all my heart.

Fat Dancer

Donna Allegra

Warm-Up

For two years I had not gone to class, ashamed of my weight gain, afraid of the contempt I expected to see masked in people's eyes. I am an African folklore and jazz dancer. In African dance forms, fat is not the crime it is in jazz dance. There's no problem with a big woman in folkloric dance, but women who strive to perform want to "look good." You know what that means. My jazz classes were harder to return to.

They are the ones where the once-over, a look up and down with the eyes, registers my weight and measurements on someone else's scale. The dreaded verdict: fat.

Isolations

I'm a compulsive overeater. I've gone from being heavy to slim to gaining weight again. I wear my hard times from food addiction and its attendant body-size obsession. Body-size obsession is a complex all unto itself. It includes the tension between the cultural dictate to be thin and the body's need to overeat in response to the strictures that tell women to look ever-slim. For most women, that look is a slenderness unnatural beyond adolescence.

Tendus

When I finally went back to classes, a West African class here, a jazz class there, having stayed away so long because I harbored such shame about my weight, I felt enormously satisfied to be back in the routine of dance. My body didn't keep me from getting back my stretch and endurance. People had missed me and welcomed me back. No one said, "Ooh, yuk, you're fat."

I had simply needed time to allow myself to live in the body I was wearing. It had served me well throughout the time of weight gain and stabilization. It didn't get in the way of my dancing, but I had cringed in chagrin against the look of it. Now I can enjoy the angles of my reflection again. Beyond that, I see how much more crucial is my need to dance. I welcome the social intimacy that develops with people in class. I crave the physical release that comes when I stretch and work my body. I savor the sweat and strain that go with dancing. If I don't nurture my dancer, I'm a very angry, unhappy girl.

Ronde de Jambes
Even more important, I could see that dance does not hinge on my body conforming to a certain size in accord with an unhealthy cultural standard for how women—women not men—are told we should look.

Pliés-Développés
I lived many years in pain, anguish, and self-rejection because I bowed down in shame to the god whose commandment is "Woman, thou shalt not be fat." The context in which I come to a hard-won self-acceptance is that of a world culture that tells me I must be slim or I won't count as an attractive contender.

Now there's a revealing word: contender. A major way that people relate to each other in this society is by competing with one another based on our looks, or attacking one another for them. A typical all-American conversation goes, "You look so good! What kind of diet are you on? Thank God I don't look like Mary: She's gained so much weight."

Turns
Men have more room to be heavy. In fact a man can be as bald as a baseball and look like he's carrying a basketball-size pregnancy, but he won't feel self-conscious about calling out his rating of the body of any woman who passes by. Sure, there's pressure on men not to commit the cardinal sin of being "too heavy," but people don't heap such fierce disdain on fat men.

Adagio
In some ways, as an African-American woman, I have a smidgen of leeway amongst my own—not a lot, but African cultures appreciate large, full-bodied women. Living in America, we're also influenced by what the dominant culture promotes as its ideals.

Other facets of racism also color the picture. As a Black woman who is often around European-Americans, I feel a particular urgency not to be the disdained, laughed-at, fat Black woman so ridiculed in white American consciousness. There's that level where white Americans project what they don't want to see in themselves as belonging to the realm of Black people. Whites are thus allowed to feel smug and superior as they discount us.

I don't want to fulfill that role. My stance here parallels why I never ate watermelon as a kid: It was expected that I would just love watermelon and grow up to be Aunt Jemima, fat and cooking happily for whites. I bridled fiercely against satisfying a stereotype no one will admit holding.

White women are kept in line by racist devices as well—their beauty measured by how much they don't look like people of color. We are said to wear the characteristics, like weight on a woman's body, that are deemed unacceptable by white American beauty standards.

Stretch on the Floor

I certainly embrace big-bodied women and have no desire to look like anything other than an African woman. I reject the "skinny blond" ideal as the only image of beauty. Still, I am unduly affected by the promotion of that imagery—Barbie, Marilyn Monroe (and she's on the heavy side according to today's standards), and *Vogue*. Even as African women are assumed to be less attractive than European women or are placed in another realm altogether for our appeal, I find it a constant struggle to view the spectrum of body types, sizes, and looks that people are born to wear and say "yes" to them all. It requires conscious effort to take in all the ways that beauty shows her colors.

And then, why this overemphasis on physical "beauty?" We are programmed to believe that attractiveness is an all-important requirement. Commercials present everything from toilet paper to motor oil in terms of how a product or style enhances our "good looks."

Center Floor

My body size has varied because of food addiction, which itself is closely coupled with body-image obsession: buying into and fighting against the slimness standard. The how-to-lose-weight appeal must be capitalism's greatest hit since sliced bread. The race to be thin sells products and services better than any angle I know.

Across the Floor

As I grapple with the culturally imposed notions that would condemn me for fat, I realize that my body size does not have the metaphoric meaning to other people that it does for me. Others may or may not judge me the way I imagine, but my body size has been the focus of internalized disapproval and self-hatred. Whatever went wrong in my life had one reference point: because I am fat.

Dance Combination

I am fat in dance classes where I once longed to be one of the slim and the small, where I gazed with longing at thinner bodies. Now I enjoy the substantial body that reflects from the mirror. I can move freely and feel my instrument sing. I fill the space with weight.

Port de Bras

I look at anorexics, whom I see more frequently in the dance world than elsewhere, and they seem to have given up their womanhood, their birth-right to flesh. They too are caged in a prison of body size, allowed only so much room to move, as was once true of me, but from a different angle in the fun-house mirror. I no longer envy them their cell.

Final Stretch

Now that I'm free from the dogma that "thin as can be" is the best body size, I can fit more smoothly into myself. I show my whole truth. I like the person who lives in this body of roundness and softness that I savor. I love the combination of muscle and fat that I see shining in the dance class mirror.

I'll probably be better able to take in the changes that come with age because of the struggle I've had to go through to get to this peace. Today my body is young and strong. Soon come that won't be true, and I'll still be the woman I am beyond the flesh, wearing a body that fits.

Applause

Dance Terms

Isolations: Exercises to warm and stretch specific body parts like the neck, shoulders, chest, and torso.

Tendus: A ballet-based warming and stretching exercise for the feet.

Ronde de jambes: Movement executed standing on one leg and drawing circles on the floor with the other leg.

Pliés-développés: Another ballet-based series of movements involving standing on one leg and balancing, while stretching the other leg from a straight to bent-knee position.

Adagio: Slow movements incorporating lessons learned through dance technique.

Across the floor: Movements done to cover distance, with a variety of steps.

Port de bras: Arm positions incorporating bows to the audience.

Nancy Barron

I Like the Me
I'm Becoming

Nancy Barron

I am fond of saying I was born nine pounds and just kept growing. I was a big baby, a big kid, a big teenager, and a big woman. "Big" means 5'10" tall, broad, and fat. Of these characteristics that do not fit the cultural ideal for women, being fat has been the most difficult.

How fat was I? Never as fat as those around me wanted me to believe, according to my pictures and present insight. I was a chubby baby and a chunky toddler, near average fatness from seven to ten, and quite fat as an early teen. At that point I was put on thyroid medication and given Dexedrine, which slimmed me to about twenty to forty pounds over the charts. Constant dieting and fasting did not hold my weight there, and, after ups and downs, both my weight and my misery peaked at 320. But for the past ten years, I have weighed 275, plus or minus ten, and have become increasingly happy.

Most of my life I was extremely unhappy with my fatness. I believed I brought it on myself, and that if I were disciplined enough, I could be thin and acceptable. I was actually a disciplined person, but as a failed dieter I often felt like a failure in everything.

That feeling started within my family, who was prejudiced against fatness and wasn't shy about making it a personal issue with me. For instance, when my new best friend from junior high came over for dinner, my dad reiterated several times his favorite litany using a nickname I hated, "Senale, you're going to bust your gut." Even as I tried to avoid committing suicide from mortification, I contemplated patricide when he pressured my friend to join in the chorus and laughter. Alternately he would call me a "bull in a china closet," which painfully insulted my burgeoning womanliness.

My mom, a hard-working farm woman, worried about her own tenaciously plump body and generally tried to "fix" me. Encouraging me to take shorter steps, keep my knees together, and soak my elbows in lemon halves so they wouldn't be dark, she took me to a doctor for the first time at age eleven. The doctor put me on my first diet. My parents loved my "sweet smile" and good grades, but they didn't love my fat.

I was also publicly harassed. Young men would drive by and hang out the car windows to yell fat obscenities at me while I walked down the sidewalk or mowed grass in my yard. Once, a man in his late twenties went out of his way to separate himself from a mixed foursome, dance up and down in front of me like a monkey, and jeer at me for looking like a "six-foot green slug" as I lounged in my green sweatshirt contemplating the ocean. This violence and the shame and rage I felt are likely familiar to any fat woman.

Yet, my fatness was not from inactivity. I remember my mom's, dad's, or teachers' voices saying in fond exasperation, "Nancy, won't you sit still?" I remember being so eager to get outdoors to play after the measles that I pulled half-completed braids out of my mother's hands. I wrestled with my father and big brothers, chased after my older siblings, romped with my little brother, roamed the hills, fields, and creeks around our farm, and rode horses (and, when no one was looking, the calves).

My fatness did affect my activity. In my country grade school, it usually took two or more friends or a much older pupil to balance me on the teeter totter. Kids quaked when I was "sent over" to break the line in Red Rover. I got a lot of guff about being the "fatty" as well as the "brain," resulting in my public bravado and private tears. In the sixth grade, another fat girl came to our small country school. She and I became friends, and that was better, not being the only one.

About this time I became excruciatingly self-conscious. Fat became the major factor in my self-concept, which was to affect my adult life with varying degrees of misery. My prepubertal growth spurt, my developmentally increasing self-awareness, my family's deprecation of fat, the trip to the doctor, the increased harassment from my peers, and the vaguely glimpsed demands of adolescent and adult female roles converged. I became convinced I was grossly fat and therefore awful. Even then, a part of my mind protested: I didn't eat when I wasn't hungry. I was being good, so why were people hassling me? My body was just growing this way, I couldn't help it.

Going to ninth grade and high school in town was saved from absolute snooldom[1] by the sports program of the YWCA—volleyball, basketball, my beloved softball—and the high school tumbling and drama clubs. Despite my fat shame and guilt, I was enthusiastic and middling good at these activities. I earned athletic letters. I played third base, catcher, and right field rather than shortstop, second base, or left field. In basketball, rebounding was not my forte, but I made baskets. I was gratified that one of the YWCA instructors was taller and fatter than I, skilled in athletics, and well-liked. Her presence lessened the minority-of-one feeling and gave me a positive model.

Camp Fire Girls camp was another positive escape from my boredom and misery. Summers from fourteen to twenty-one I spent happily teaching horseback riding (wrangling my own string of seven to nine horses) and sometimes water activities. When riding, I chose larger horses and improvised a mounting block when feasible. My skills were valued and my size generally ignored. I felt good about myself in that setting. The emotional crunch came at counselors' night out after camp closing and cleanup, when we all donned hose and heels and went out for a formal dinner. Then I felt behemoth and alien.

During my childhood, my major wounds were the lack of support from my family and the public and the resulting damage to my self-esteem. My high natural activity level and my generally "uppity" nature helped me retain good physical and mental health. Although I believed my size was a severe disadvantage in the interpersonal and social scene in high school, my extracurricular sports, drama, and camp experiences were graced by women who worked with me, taking my size into account. Their support created bright spots of sunshine in an otherwise dark emotional landscape and allowed me to build the foundation for my later positive self-regard and self-acceptance. I thank them.

Finally, as a college student, my intelligence became an asset socially, and I didn't have to worry about being teased about being a "brain." My physical activity, though, was still not okay. In the 1950s, women's athletics or fitness had little status or acceptability, even on a liberal arts campus focusing on personal development and requiring physical education. I felt apologetic and vaguely ashamed of my pull to be active. Real women didn't sweat—or be strong, agile, and goal-directed. Nonetheless, still living at home on the farm, I had riding and walking; on campus I had swimming and team sports to fit around my studies and social life; and summers I had my beloved camp.

When I lived in Germany on a Fulbright scholarship, *man lauft immer*— one always walks. The Germans esteemed my activity and my substantial body. Although I immersed myself in the German culture, I perpetuated my American fat phobia by continuing to diet.

Back in the States, the automobile, the grueling hours of work and graduate study, and "appropriate" adult roles took over. Ambivalently, I became a wife who cooked. I became more and more sedentary, and my weight and my misery inched up. After the boost to my self-confidence from my first position as a professional psychologist, I once more gathered my determination and lost weight on the "Air Force Diet." When I resumed normal eating, I quickly regained the forty pounds, hating myself every ounce of the way. I tried analytic psychotherapy and behavior modification to no avail.

I gained weight as I stopped smoking, as I drove and flew around Missouri developing evaluations for mental health programs, and as I had three babies. After a back operation, muscle spasms severely hampered my movement, which repeatedly initiated days of lying on the floor despite trying to manage toddlers. I gained more weight. No matter what exercise I tried, I couldn't get started slowly and gently enough not to cause another crisis with my back. As I passed 300 pounds, I felt hopelessly like the fat lady in the circus.

As a psychology student, as a psychologist, or as a client in the 1950s, 60s, and 70s, I experienced major strain between what I was learning about fatness and what I was experiencing as a fat woman. I had a Ph.D., a demanding job, and a young family, proving I was not without willpower in my daily life. (In fact, if I had had less willpower and stoicism and paid attention to my family history of back trouble, I might have treated my back earlier instead of pushing through the pain and necessitating an operation.) I was not dumb, lazy, greedy. I was neither sexually repressed nor a nymphomaniac. I was not a compulsive eater (although I suffered from occasional mild binges). I was simply hungry. My lifelong low blood sugar had not been diagnosed, but I knew I needed to eat often, despite lifelong admonitions to "just cut out snacks" and the social sneer often elicited in response to a fat woman eating, especially at an "inappropriate" time. I didn't work right without a certain amount of fuel. Dieting made me feel bad. I simply gained more weight when I went off a diet. Everyone hoorayed my weight losses—I couldn't figure out why they cared more about my smaller size than my well-being.

My physical turnaround came from belly dancing with a feminist teacher, which brought back my flexibility. I had to fight through memories of fat woman's abuse to allow myself the experience of moving my body. What joy to experience being in my body! I discovered a wholeness. I felt grounded and playful in my embodied spirit. My ankles, knees, trunk muscles, and arms felt stronger. So did my self-confidence. I always feel better after dancing.

The emotional turnaround came in Fat Group.[2] In 1978 I was Chair of Woman's Place, a small, feminist, non-profit organization that developed workshops, sisterhood support suppers and networks, consciousness-raising groups, and a feminist bookstore. Jeanne, another board member, had heard that a radical social worker from Berkeley who had worked with Alan Dolit[3] in fat liberation was coming to town. We engaged Louise to join us for six weeks to launch a self-help group for fat women.[4]

The group lasted two years, until several of us moved. During this group, I concluded that dieting was cruel and unusual punishment and that I would never do that to myself again. I began to believe my internal reality, and I had glimmers of how important it was to affirm that reality publicly instead of remaining silent or denying it. Instead of avoiding being seen with other fat women for fear people would sneer about "those losers," I began to seek their company, learning about their courage and interesting journeys. Hot tubbing together, eating together, and belly dancing together deepened the healing of our emotional sharing.

I quit dieting. I focused on building myself a quality eating experience— I would eat when hungry, stop when full (most of the time), and enjoy every calorie to its utmost. I no longer bolted my food so I wouldn't have time to make myself stop before I was full. The semiconscious state that I had used to numb the guilt and punishment for eating too much gave way to the full awareness of the rightness of eating. I became active again, even though I felt huge. I worked in individual therapy with Louise. I became more politicized around fatness.

My fat activism sprang from my ten-year involvement in the women's movement, especially my consciousness-raising group, the OWLs (Older Women's Liberationists). The group itself had not been particularly enlightened about fatness. However, it had been an oasis of sanity, validation, and friendship in a world of nuclear family dynamics and public mental health bureaucracy. These dear women cared about me rather than my roles, public faces, or body size. I processed with them how I think I'm shouting my feelings yet others can sometimes barely hear me. These women supported my expressing my feelings and clarifying my feminist values. They encouraged me to believe in my own perceptions and experiences, and cheered me on in accepting myself and going for my goals.

Then Oregon called me to north woods, ocean, and the mountains and to new age social values more compatible with me than those of the midwestern bible belt. Between passionate trips to the coast for this ocean-deprived midwesterner and a job in self-help group research that drew me strongly, I looked for fat groups and belly dancing, and found none.

Seeking a fat group too, Barbara found me through my job. She and I found several other women to join us in creating a fat women's self-help group. My most salient memory of the group is realizing that I loved a woman, managing my divorce (long in the making), and coming out as a lesbian—not what the group was about at all, but tremendously enhancing to my body image.[5]

Barbara and I next began a self-help group through the YWCA, planning to (1) foster member leadership in the group so it would continue after our few months were over, (2) combine physical activity pleasant and appropriate for fat women (swims, walks, dancing, etc.) with verbal support and consciousness-raising, and (3) nurture the ability for fat women to integrate their verbal and body awareness through talking together about the experience of moving. The group has survived as a support group; however, participating in physical activities and talking about them quickly fell away. I continue to find that the ability to talk about the physical and emotional experience of movement is very difficult for women.

During this time, the early 1980s, material was coming out that empirically supported my philosophy and experience, for example *The Dieter's Dilemma*[6] and *Shadow on a Tightrope*[7]. Barbara and I then wanted to start a small feminist business for the health, happiness, and empowerment of fat women. We wanted the business to have the flexibility to seduce women into regaining the pleasure of moving, allow women safe and supportive space, maximize personal growth, and act as a base for political and social action against fat phobia. I put up "mom money" (a bit of family inheritance), and we wrote a letter to all the fat women we knew describing our intended action and asked them to come together and consult with us. Thus was Ample Opportunity born.[8]

Ample Opportunity has been a complex process for me. We set it up to structure our lives in positive directions, benefiting all of us who developed and facilitated it and the women who came to take part in activities. Much of the time, we were successful.

During early Ample Opportunity (1983-85) I was coming out as a fat woman. This closely followed my coming out as a lesbian, and I was aware of the parallels. (It's not that I think that one has to be a lesbian to be a fat activist, or that all fat activists are lesbian, but that a similar process was involved in coming out as a fat woman and as a lesbian. But, fearing that many fat women couldn't handle scary feelings about both fatness and lesbians, I was quiet about being a lesbian in Ample Opportunity circles. Taking a stand against oppression of homosexuals proposed by Oregon's recently defeated Measure 9 brought me more fully out.)

First, I acknowledged to myself that I was fat—probably permanently, that I was really me, and that it was okay. Then, I clarified my feelings and values and began to translate them into behavior. I tried to let others in my life know that it was not okay to oppress me or other fat women and that diets do infinitely more harm than good to both body and soul. I tried to educate people about the experiences and facts about fatness and dispel the myths.

Next, I tried to be a positive model and to engender hope and enthusiasm for a physically and mentally healthy, active lifestyle for fat women. It was important to me to be a model and encourage activism toward equitable access to societal rewards such as approval, employment, seat belts, and stylish clothes that fit.

I also think that coming out as a lesbian gave me strength to dare to begin Ample Opportunity. I acknowledged my woman-identified nature. I removed myself enough from the patriarchal misogyny underlying fat phobia to gather strength to publicly break taboos and challenge myths about fatness. Though I quickly had to give up the myth that lesbians were all supportive, I did get a great deal of encouragement and support from the lesbians in my life.

Just becoming an activist didn't instantly make me size-acceptant. When things threatened to overwhelm me, the voice inside my head would join the harassment: "Fat slob, they're right, you know." Then I had to work my way out of that depressed mood by using my own feelings and experiences as the touchstone of my reality. I often felt on the raw edge, disclosing my realities, including pain at the injustice, and getting a blame-the-victim response. I was labeled an enabler of unhealthy lifestyles. How ironic it was, when my Ample Opportunity efforts were precisely the opposite—to enable fat women to achieve greater health and happiness. But I continued to differentiate between personal experience and social constructions, which did foster my increasing personal acceptance of my size.

When I began my activism, the concept of size acceptance had not yet been created. Many people stared at me blankly when I described my approach and Ample Opportunity. *A weight-loss group, right?* No. *A support group, then?* Partly, and much more. *Like AA?* No, fatness is more a matter of the body type you're born with rather than an addiction. *You mean, you think it's all right to be fat??* Yes, and some people just are. *You're enabling dysfunction, you know, and rationalizing your own failure.* No, I'm enabling good people to live good lives, beginning with me.

My beliefs in a fat-positive feminist organization were tested. Barbara left Ample Opportunity and entered graduate school, the advisory council disbanded, volunteers disappeared without warning, men left obscene messages on the Ample Opportunity phone line, etc. I had to keep putting in money to run the program, yet at one point was accused of pocketing all the profits despite having open books. But women kept coming to the organization and finding its philosophy freeing and empowering.

Then Johanna Brenner, head of Women's Studies at Portland State University, recruited me to develop and teach a summer course on Self-Image and Body Size. Soon co-listed in psychology, sociology, and health, this course became financially self-sufficient through Extended Studies, which allowed a constant flow of students to take the course despite lack of budget. The course brought together many women and some men to study and experience the transition possible from fat phobia to size acceptance.

University teaching helped me structure time to keep current in the burst of new information about the dynamics of fatness and fat phobia and lent academic credibility to my efforts, which I found satisfying. Teaching allowed me time to discuss issues intellectually and scientifically (in addition to the more growth-oriented discussions of Ample Opportunity). I became profoundly convinced that fat phobia damages not only fat women, but also all women, and that every man, woman, and child in our society would be better off without this phobia.

This realization steadied me in my fat activism and broadened my Ample Opportunity efforts. I kept going despite burnout from a full-time job in public mental health, my class, and Ample Opportunity. I persevered because of my convictions and my increasing personal experience that "A good life is the best revenge." I was stronger, healthier, and happier following Ample Opportunity premises. And, finally, size acceptance was becoming a concept some people knew. I got to know colleagues: Susan Wooley, who asked if obesity *should* be treated; Jane Moore, thin proponent of fit and fat[9]; Jann Mitchell, editor of the Living section of the *Oregonian* newspaper; Marcia Hutchinson, author of *Transforming Body Image*; Pat Lyons and Debby Burgard, authors of *Great Shape: The First Fitness Guide for Large Women*; Alice Ansfield, editor of *Radiance* magazine; Etta Martin, therapist and activist; and Joe McVoy, originator of the Mountain Lake size-acceptance conferences and the Association for the Health Enrichment of Large People. Knowing these people brought a sense of kinship and delighted excitement.

The support of my friends and partner nourished me. My family life was transformed. In my family of origin, there was active harassment. My husband loved me in spite of my weight and learned not to interfere in the name of helping. My first lesbian partner expressed neutrality about my weight and worked with me toward fat positiveness. Sara acknowledges that my build is part of what draws her toward me. She supports my Ample Opportunity efforts, and, as a natural mountain goat, shows great patience with my more Clydesdale nature as we share some of our outdoor activities, though differently abled. Our grown kids support my size-acceptance work. I think my daughter, who is built a lot like me, is proud of the work. For my family to love who I am, including my fatness and how I act regarding it, increases my acceptance of my fatness.

Ample Opportunity has incorporated, and though I am still president, a board of women dear to me own the organization. It thrives, and some of my most profound satisfactions are seeing the relief and excitement of Ample Opportunity women as they discover that they are okay as they are and that they can do things they never thought possible. I have resumed practicing as a therapist part-time, which also offers opportunity to use Ample Opportunity precepts.

At fifty-three, I am still trying to learn that gradual building of strength and activity is more effective than heroic efforts. I'm proud I learned to cross-country ski, fat and fifty, and I'm so pleased I had two days in a row of skiing last weekend. My canoe is the nicest gift my daughter ever gave me. T'ai Chi is a comforting, centering delight that leaves me with more flexible knees and strength. I experienced the magic of the Great Barrier Reef last winter through my first scuba dive. I happily swam and snorkeled two or three times a day. I'm looking forward to teaching belly dance again this spring. The active small girl within me is so much happier now that I allow her out to play instead of telling her to sit still. Making time and space for her to move amidst all the work is a constant goal for the grown-ups in me.

But it's not easy. I still work too hard. Size acceptance is still an uphill climb for me as well as the rest of the world. I occasionally think that if everything comes together, I'll get thinner, or that some new supplement may help me lose a few—not.

Keeping up is my current growing edge. Our household enjoys outdoor sports, but family members are all some combination of younger, stronger, faster, fitter. Guess who's the cow's tail in all the family activities? But competition is the least of the issues. Wanting not to spoil their fun, wanting not to be the limiting factor, wanting them to want to go with me, and wanting not to push myself so hard that it's painful or causes injuries sometimes preoccupy me when I could be enjoying the sunset or the trail.

The situation involves issues of personal power and choice. Heaven knows I would like to be able to do more at Sara's level. Doing some things together, though, means she has to do them at my more limited pace. We have to make sure she has a chance to do things her way as well, so we have become ingenious at staging outings. For instance, I let Sara out at one end of a trail segment, drive around to the other end, and walk in to meet her. This solution gives both her and me time alone at our own pace (and solves the transportation problem). After walking about twice as far as I, she is more ready to do the rest together at my slower pace. We also choose easy ski trails with adjoining more difficult loops for her, or she goes up and down a particularly sweet bit twice while I do it once.

I also pay attention to keeping my own head screwed on right, not letting my internal taskmaster berate and harass me for not being more able than I am. I focus on keeping my goals relevant to my ability. I tune my senses to the beauty and joy of the experience and close out the performance ethic dithers.

Another growing edge for me is speaking truth. I don't mean I lie. I mean I'm sometimes still afraid deep down in my gut that "they" (general or specific) will punish me if I break the taboos by talking about the realities of being a fat woman and advocating for my/our worth. Naming the fat experience challenges the reigning beliefs; there are social repercussions for violating powerful taboos. I felt such a sense of relief and kinship when Susan Wooley asked during the first Mountain Lake size-acceptance conference, "When I speak of my woman's experience, why do I feel like I'm lying?"[10]

We have been taught to feel guilty and wrong in voicing our reality. Over the last decade, I have become much more adept at naming the experience whether it fits fat stereotypes or female stereotypes or jostles the social phobias—gynephobia, fat phobia, homophobia. Speaking has become easier; it is still difficult to commit such thoughts to paper. Writing for the

Ample Opportunity newsletter, *Ample Information*, has helped. I look forward to my writing becoming clearer as I control this dragon. (Dragons may be immortal, but, as I see it, mine shrink to a nubbin and pale to insignificance when my authenticity and vitality are high.)

Mostly I'm happy with the sensual/sexual depths of me, the comfortable clothes enveloping me, my out-front role in fat activism, new outdoor sports each year, my many aspects as a psychologist, my precious relationships, and my growing edges. If I had to account for what I have done in my life that is useful, my most meaningful accomplishments would include my personal and community efforts toward size acceptance.

[1] Snooldom: The state in which snools rule, and snools are the rule. Snool: Normal inhabitant of sadosociety characterized by sadism and masochism combined (Daly, M. and Caputi, J., *Webster's First New Intergalactic Wickedary*, Beacon, 1987).

[2] Barron, N., Eakins, L.I., and Wollert, R., "Fat Group: A SNAP-Launched Self-Help Group for Overweight Women," *Human Organization, 43*, pp. 44-49, 1984.

[3] Dolit, A., *Fat Liberation: The Awareness Technique*, Celestial Arts, 1974.

[4] Pietrafesa, L.C. and Barron, N., "SNAP-Launched Self-Help Groups: Power to Overweight Women," Paper presented at the American Psychological Association Annual Convention, New York, September 1979.

[5] Nancy is currently working on a paper, "My Lesbian Body," for *Lesbian Body Image* edited by D. Atkins.

[6] Bennett, William, M.D. and Gurin, Joel, *The Dieter's Dilemma: The Scientific Case Against Dieting as a Means of Weight Control*, Basic Books, 1982.

[7] Schoenfielder, Lisa and Wieser, Barb, *Shadow on a Tightrope: Writings by Women on Fat Oppression*, Aunt Lute Book Company, 1983.

[8] Barron, N. and Lear, B.H., "Ample Opportunity for Women," *Women and Therapy, 8*, pp. 79-92, 1989.

[9] Women Can Be Both Fit and Fat, Oregon Study Shows," *Los Angeles Times*, part II, p. 5, June 27, 1988.

[10] Wooley, S., "Obesity Treatment: Broken Promises and Lost Opportunities," Paper presented at the conference, Alternative Approaches to Treating Obesity in the 90s, at Mountain Lake, Virginia, March 1991.

Judith Parker

Both Sides Now

Judith Parker

I've looked at life from both sides now,
from up and down and still somehow
It's life's illusion I recall,
I really don't know life at all.

—from "Clouds" by Joni Mitchell

I first heard the word *fat* applied to me when I was about five years old. My daddy had gone to South America to work and left my mother and me to ramble around an old mansion in a small Kansas town. The pictures of me from this time show a chubby, wistful little girl, a big difference from the carefree abandon apparent in earlier pictures. Despite the obvious shift in my feeling state, only my body was attended to or mentioned.

My life proceeded—up and down—and all anyone ever commented on was the size of my body. I was good when I was thin (I don't remember being in this state long enough to become familiar with it), bad when I was fat. How I felt, what was going on inside me went unnamed, not a suitable topic for discussion.

So I grew up with a great deal of shame in my body and not a clue about who I was or what I was feeling. My life swung between the two poles of being accepted as a body or rejected as a body. I interpreted all my experience from this perspective. If I was thin, I was accepted and everything was fine. If I was fat, I was repulsive and rejected, I was awful. I thought I controlled this pendulum by dieting.

By the time I was thirty-eight, I was tired of swinging to the tune of other people's evaluations of me. I was angry at having to do this dance that never let me rest. I realized how out of control I was of my own happiness. It was 1984, both my parents were dead, and I felt free to pursue my truth instead of everyone else's. I created a crisis to cure me.

I had been in Jungian analysis for five years with a white-haired, wise old man. Amazingly, the subject of my body had never come up. In search of acceptance and safety, I had earned a Ph.D. and related almost exclusively as a talking head. One day, out of the blue, I asked my analyst if he found me attractive.

He was quiet for a moment, then said, "This is embarrassing. I'm not attracted to you because of your weight." His answer devastated me. This answer was the theme of my life, the words I had spent my life running from. My worst fear had happened, which I now know is always a liberating event.

For a few moments I felt the pain of his and my own deeper rejection, then suddenly a new feeling bubbled up—rage! I spluttered something about how people are "of a piece" and how crazy-making it is to hear, from childhood on, that people would love and accept you if only you looked differently.

After I left his office I started to ponder what motivations could have prompted him to bring up the size of my body in response to my question. Instead of feeling ashamed of my size, my self, as I had always done in the past, I began to consider the new question of what his comment revealed about him. My fantasy was that if I were thin, he would focus on some other supposed imperfection in my appearance to justify his rejection. From what I knew of his personal life, he was critical of his wife's body, though she was a perfectly attractive woman in her fifties. It was my father's rejection and criticism of me and my mother—all in the nutshell of that therapeutic encounter. It was wonderful and horrible!

I wanted to talk to a woman who could support me in this new perspective, but couldn't think of one who wasn't on a diet or feeling she should be. I guessed that perhaps a black woman wouldn't be so hung up on white men's body standards, but I didn't know one well enough to discuss such a vulnerable issue. I vowed to start a group for other women trying to find the support necessary to reclaim their natural bodies. My journal entry on that day, the first day of summer, read in part:

For my whole life I have felt crazy and deformed but today I got in touch with my anger at a man and a society that sets such unnatural standards for women. I feel more attractive than I ever have. A new attitude has been born.

In the months and years that followed, I went from never mentioning my body size in polite company to speaking publicly about my experiences and ideas about body image and self-esteem on radio and television and in person. I dared to do things I had never had the confidence to do, like riding horses, taking and teaching dance classes, and having glamour photographs taken by a professional. I spent a lot of money on bold clothing that made me feel beautiful.

I wrote and thought a lot of about the self-acceptance process. One of my wild ideas was the possibility that by accepting myself at my current weight, I might lose weight. I loved the paradox of this idea. I can see in retrospect that this fantasy is not one of a woman who has really accepted herself.

Interestingly enough, this prophesied weight loss did come to pass. In the summer of 1987, two weeks before an extended trip to Europe, I was thrown while riding a horse and broke my right arm. I had dared to reach for too much happiness and I couldn't bear it. My arm was in a cast for ten weeks, during which time I gained ten pounds. When the cast came off, I started a course of body work and deep healing to regain the use of my arm. As part of that healing I saw a nutritionist, not to lose weight, but to identify foods that would maximize my energy and allow me to feel my best. Over the next two years I slowly, almost imperceptibly, lost forty pounds. The primary change in my diet was avoiding wheat, which I found I was allergic to. Although I still exceeded the weights on the insurance tables, at 190 pounds, I really didn't feel like a large woman.

I had been thinner in my life but never before had I had such a realistic positive body image. I felt terrific! I started doing large-size modeling in addition to my work as a psychologist. What a lark! I got paid fifty to seventy dollars an hour just to try on beautiful clothing tailor-made for me. My body was finally the standard for thousands of women, a perfect size eighteen.

As usual it came as a shock to realize that life wasn't perfect with less flesh on my bones. During that period a man I was very attracted to rejected me, and my feelings of shame and humiliation were the same ones I had always associated with being fat. I had the feelings without the flesh. This situation made me stop and look deeply into these feelings of shame connected with my body. I discovered that I had been sexually abused as a very young child.

Knowing I had been violated as a child helped me understand the pain of my life far better than the fat=bad and thin=good interpretation I had been using. I had taken all the guilt onto myself, and my body weight had become the indicator of my sin. I worked hard to bless and affirm myself in the knowledge that my weight had nothing to do with my value and goodness. This work improved my self-esteem tremendously.

Then I started to encounter problems associated with being too thin. I lost modeling jobs because I wasn't big enough! What irony! I encountered prejudice from larger women in the size-acceptance community. The implication was that I was not really large and therefore didn't understand the problem. I realized that I had had a vested interest in being a large woman. At one time after I decided to accept myself, I felt sorry for thinner women. I could now see in the attitudes of my bigger sisters that it was just as wrong to hold fat as an ideal as it was to hold thin as the ideal. Women should be free to be any size!

I started feeling the disapproval I always thought was associated with being too large. True to my history, I let that disapproval rule my life. I knew it all had been too good to be true and the success was making me very uncomfortable. I felt envy from some of my closest friends. I didn't feel safe at all. I had felt this way before my extended trip to Europe, when

I chose the safe prison of a broken arm over the disconcerting exhilaration of living life on my own terms.

I arranged my demise this time by becoming involved with a man who was a spiritual vampire, a goodwill ambassador for the walking wounded. Thin as a rail himself, he loved junk food of all kinds, especially pizza. We spent lots of time together, eventually living together. We ate all our meals together. I let him talk me into meals, and other things, I knew would disagree with me. For the first six months of this regimen my weight stayed stable. When I became increasingly worried about what I was eating and the eventual effect on my weight, the numbers on the scale started to rise. To be brief, I separated from this man after another six months and by then I was the proud owner of the forty pounds I had lost before.

The following year was a dark one for me. I had to come to terms with being 44 years old, being without a lover or gainful employment, and being fat—all my worst fears. This time strengthened me. I had to come face to face with myself because I had nothing to hide behind. I came out of this experience knowing and valuing myself more.

This year has been a good one. I am starting to support myself in living my dreams. I am leaving soon to go to Hawaii, the new home I envision for myself. I will stay for one month, the longest time I have ever given myself off in my adult life. I have become my own best friend. I realize my value and beauty have nothing to do with my weight. I am leading a body-acceptance and self-esteem support group for women. The women in it are of various sizes. Amazingly, we all feel or have felt the same way about ourselves and the size and shape of our bodies. We were all sexually abused as children. We are in varying stages of realizing that our bodies are our own and that the purpose of life is not earning approval, but living fully. We are struggling to be our best creative selves and to be valued and supported for who we are. I believe we are all trying to feel entitled to take up as much space as we please in life. As someone who has been on both sides now, I can offer them a vision that sees right through the flesh and into the spiritual necessity of becoming oneself.

Contributor Notes

Donna Allegra has published poetry, fiction, and essays in *Sinister Wisdom*, *Common Lives/Lesbian Lives*, *Conditions*, *Sojourner*, *Aché*, and other lesbian-feminist journals. Her work has also appeared in three anthologies published by The Crossing Press: *Finding the Lesbians, The Original Coming Out Stories*, and *Lesbian Love Stories, Vol. 2*. Donna lives in New York City.

Nancy Barron, Ph.D., is a psychologist in Portland, Oregon. She is a private practitioner, a Program Evaluation Specialist for the Mental and Emotional Disabilities Program of Multnomah County, and an Assistant Professor at Portland State University. She is the founder and president of Ample Opportunity, a nonprofit health and empowerment organization for fat women.

Bernadette Lynn Bosky studied English literature at Duke University's graduate school and now combines or alternates teaching and writing. The topics of her nonfiction range from science fiction to renaissance alchemy, Stephen King to self-esteem. Her most recent work is a piece of science fiction erotica with a fat protagonist for Circlet Press. She lives a deceptively quiet suburban life in Yonkers, New York, with her partners, Arthur Hlavaty and Kevin Maroney.

Debbie Bowling is a writer, editor, and video producer living in Atlanta, Georgia.

Patricia Cominos is a poet and writer living in Catskill, New York. Her poems have been published in *The Washout Review*, other literary magazines, and *Cosmopolitan*. She is currently working on her first novel, *See How They Shine*.

Diane M. Ceja is a registered dietitian with a Master's degree in public health nutrition. She loves working with children and writing. Diane lives in Berkeley, California, with her husband and two daughters.

Dixie Colvin is a freelance writer, screenwriter, and workshop leader who lives in Albuquerque, New Mexico, and plays around the world. Deeply spiritual, she has discovered the only way to healing is to open her heart and allow the love in and out.

Debra Derr lives in Parsippany, New Jersey, and publishes the litzine (i.e., literary magazine) *tiny lion* with her husband, artist David Derr.

Jane Dwinell is the author of *Birth Stories: Mystery, Power, and Creation* (Bergin and Garvey, 1992). She lives, writes, and homesteads in the Northeast Kingdom of Vermont, where she is at work on her second book, *Self-Reliance and Voluntary Simplicity*.

Barbara Elder is a writer, mother, and fat chick, among other talents. She lives in Santa Cruz, California, with her husband, Lee, their perfect daughter, Alix, and an ill-tempered cat called Elmo. They are all currently living happily ever after.

Sara Greer lives in Seattle, Washington, with her husband and their spoiled, elderly cat. She has worked at a variety of jobs to support her writing habit and still enjoys disconcerting doctors.

Patt Jackson is owner/operator of a small service business and a freelance writer who lives in Duluth, Minnesota. She attributes her sanity and good fortune to a loving family and two feline housemates. This is her first published essay.

Pat Kite is a Newark, California, politician, writer, teacher, people advocate, and mother. She raised four now-grown children as a single parent, and she credits her success to friends, persistence, and an occasional Snickers bar.

Rosemary E. Knox lives in Gresham, Oregon.

Diana Lambson is a California native now living in Stamford, Nebraska (188 souls strong). Actively involved in her local Lutheran church, the Nebraska Synod E.L.C.A, Red Cross, several community organizations, and two writers' groups, she is also a correspondent for the Hastings Tribune, a regional daily newspaper, and a freelance writer/poet. She and her husband, Ivan, of 24 years have two children, Marlis Lynn, 23, and Trevor Lee, 16.

Randi Ward Mochamer is a teacher living in Elkhart, Indiana.

Judith Parker, Ph.D., is a psychologist and currently a full-bodied woman who is actively engaged in the process of loving herself and others. She has written a soon-to-be published book, *Women with Nothing to Lose*. You can contact her by calling 1-800-597-BODY.

Gail Picado is a native Californian, with two daughters and one grand-daughter. Gail began writing at age 36 and her goal is to write children's stories that adults will find nostalgic. She has also written and self-published her father's biography, *No One's Son*.

Jody Savage has a Master's in cell biology and is a one-person Regulatory Affairs Department at a San Francisco Bay area biotechnology company. Jody lives with her life partner, three children, two dogs, a cat, and a parakeet. The hamster, alas, has escaped.

Katharine Schneider lives and loves in Eugene, Oregon. Living includes teaching and social work. Loving includes her friends, her writing, and her body.

DeAnn G. Semler is a graduate of Clarke College in Dubuque, Iowa, and Lesley College in Cambridge, Massachusetts. She has an MA in writing. She is a native Iowan and is currently living in Seattle, Washington, with her partner James Flack. DeAnn's hobbies include science fiction, volunteering for the Phinney Neighborhood Center, and developing her talents as a stand-up comedian.

Sondra Solovay is an adventurer born in an alternate universe. She stepped through a tear in the space-time continuum. She is currently using performance art, political activism, sculpture, the study of law, and playwriting to contribute to the social advancement of Earthlings until she can return to her planet.

Lou Ann Thomas has been a professional journalist as well as a high school English and journalism teacher. Lou Ann lives outside of Lawrence, Kansas, where she writes and provides a home for her cats, Harry and Emily.

Fiona Webster is a psychiatrist and writer living in Greenbelt, Maryland. Her personal essays, criticism, and book reviews focus on the darker aspects of life and art. She writes a column on horror fiction for *The Reading Edge*, and is active in the Internet community.

Carol A. Wiley is a writer, editor, martial artist, and contact improvisation dancer living in Bellevue, Washington. She is the editor of *Women in the Martial Arts* published by North Atlantic Books and *Journeys to Self-Acceptance: Fat Women Speak* published by The Crossing Press.

Further Reading

Books

Atrens, Dale M., Ph.D., *Don't Diet*, William Morrow and Company, 1988.

Beller, Ann Scott, *Fat and Thin—A Natural History of Obesity*, Farrar, Strauss and Giroux, 1977.

Bennett, William, M.D., and Joel Gurin, *The Dieter's Dilemma: Eating Less and Weighing More*, Basic Books, 1982.

Bringle, Mary Louise, *The God of Thinness: Gluttony and Other Weighty Matters*, Abingdon Press, 1992.

Brown, Laura S., and Esther Rothblum, Ph.D., Ed's., *Overcoming Fear of Fat*, Harrington Park Press, 1989.

Cash, Thomas F., and Thomas Pruzinsky, Ed's., *Body Image: Development, Deviance, and Change*, The Guilford Press, 1990.

Chernin, Kim, *The Hungry Self: Women, Eating, and Identity*, Times Books, 1985.

Chernin, Kim, *The Obsession: Reflections on the Tyranny of Slenderness*, Perennial Library, Harper and Row, 1982.

Ciliska, Donna, R.N., Ph.D., *Beyond Dieting, Psychoeducational Interventions for Chronically Obese Women: A Non-Dieting Approach*, Brunner/Mazel Inc., 1990.

Freedman, Rita, Ph.D., *Bodylove: Learning to Like Our Looks—and Ourselves*, Harper and Row, 1989.

Garrison, Terry Nicholetti, with David Levitsky, Ph.D., *Fed Up! A Woman's Guide to Freedom from the Diet/Weight Prison*, Carroll & Graf, 1993.

Higgs, Liz Curtis, *One Size Fits All and Other Fables*, Thomas Nelson Books, 1993.

Hutchinson, Marcia Germaine, Ed.D., *Transforming Body Image: Learning to Love the Body You Have*, The Crossing Press, 1985.

Kano, Susan, *Making Peace With Food*, Amity Publishing Co., 1985.

Lyons, Pat, R.N., and Debby Burgard, *Great Shape: The First Exercise Guide for Large Women*, Arbor House, William Morrow and Company, 1988.

Millman, Marcia, *Such a Pretty Face: Being Fat in America*, W.W. Norton and Company, 1980.

Olds, Ruthanne, *Big and Beautiful: How to Be Gorgeous on Your Own Grand Scale*, Acropolis Books Ltd., 1984.

Polivy, Janet, and C. Peter Herman, *Breaking the Diet Habit: The Natural Weight Alternative*, Basic Books, 1983.

Roberts, Nancy, *Breaking All the Rules*, Penguin Books, 1985.

Rodin, Dr. Judith, *Body Traps: Breaking the Binds That Keep You From Feeling Good About Your Body*, William Morrow and Company, 1992.

Schoenfielder, Lisa, and Barb Wieser, *Shadow on a Tightrope: Writings by Women on Fat Oppression*, Aunt Lute Book Company, 1983.

Schroeder, Charles Roy, Ph.D., *Fat Is Not a Four-Letter Word*, Chronimed Publishing, 1992.

Seid, Roberta Pollack, *Never Too Thin: Why Women Are at War With Their Bodies*, Prentice Hall Press, 1989.

Schwartz, Hillel, *Never Satisfied: A Cultural History of Diets, Fantasies, and Fat*, The Free Press, 1986.

Shaw, Carole, and Hank Huwer, *Come Out, Come Out, Wherever You Are*, American R.R. Publishing Company, 1982.

Wolf, Naomi, *The Beauty Myth: How Images of Beauty Are Used Against Women*, William Morrow and Company, 1991.

Articles

Attie, Ilana, and J. Brooks-Gunn, "Weight Concerns as Chronic Stressors in Women," in *Gender and Stress*, edited by Rosalind C. Barnett, Lois Biener, and Grace K. Baruch, The Free Press, 1987.

Brody, Jane E., "For Most Trying to Lose Weight, Dieting Only Makes Things Worse," *New York Times*, November 23, 1992, p. A1.

Ernsberger, Paul, and Paul Haskew, "Rethinking Obesity: An Alternative View of its Health Implications," a monograph issue of *The Journal of Obesity and Weight Reduction*, Human Sciences Press, Summer 1987.

Hall, Trish, "Diet Pills Return as Long-Term Medication, Not Just Diet Aids," *New York Times*, October 14, 1992.

Haynes, R. B., "Is Weight Loss an Effective Treatment for Hypertension? The Evidence Against," *Canadian Journal of Physiology and Pharmacology*, Vol. 64, 1986, p. 825 (6).

Kolata, Gina, "The Burdens of Being Overweight: Mistreatment and Misconceptions," *New York Times*, November 22, 1992, p. A1.

Lyons, Pat, "Fat and Fit: An Idea Whose Time Has Come," *The Network News*, May-June 1992, p. 1 (4).

National Institutes of Health, "Methods for Voluntary Weight Loss and Control: Technology Assessment Conference Statement," *Nutrition Today*, July-August 1992, p. 27 (7).

O'Neill, Molly, "A Growing Movement Fights Diets Instead of Fat," *New York Times*, April 12, 1992, p. 1.

Polivy, Janet, and C. Peter Herman, "Diagnosis and Treatment of Normal Eating," *Journal of Consulting and Clinical Psychology*, Vol. 55, October 1987, p. 635 (9).

Polivy, Janet, and C. Peter Herman, "Undieting: A Program to Help People Stop Dieting," *International Journal of Eating Disorders*, April 1992, p. 261 (8).

Riley, Karen, "Three Diet Programs Agree to Stop Making Claims They Can't Prove," *The Washington Times*, October 17, 1991, p. C1.

Rosenthal, Elisabeth, "Commercial Diets Lack Proof of Their Long-Term Success," *New York Times*, November 24, 1992, p. A1.

Tisdale, Sally, "A Weight That Women Carry," *Harper's Magazine*, March 1993, p. 49 (5). An article on self-acceptance by a moderately large woman.

United States Congress, House Committee on Small Business, Subcommittee on Regulation, Business Opportunities, and Energy, *Deception and Fraud in the Diet Industry*, One Hundred First Congress, Second Session, Washington DC, 1990.

Watts, Nelson B., Robert G. Spanheimer, Mario DiGirolamo, Suzanne S. P. Gebhart, Victoria C. Musey, Y. Khalid Siddiq, and Lawerence S. Phillips, "Prediction of Glucose Response to Weight Loss in Patients with Non-Insulin-Dependent Diabetes Mellitus," *Archives of Internal Medicine*, April 1990, p. 803 (4).

Weigle, David S., "Human Obesity: Exploding the Myths," *The Western Journal of Medicine*, October 1990, p. 421 (8).

Wooley, Susan C., and Orland W. Wooley, "Should Obesity Be Treated At All?" in *Eating and Its Disorders*, edited by Albert J. Stunkard and Eliot Stellar, Raven Press, 1984.

Resources

National Association to Advance Fat Acceptance (NAAFA)
P.O. Box 188620
Sacramento, CA 95818

Council on Size and Weight Discrimination
P.O. Box 238
Columbia, MD 21045

Association for the Health Enrichment of Large People
P.O. Drawer C
Radford, VA 24143

Radiance: The Magazine for Large Women
P.O. Box 30246
Oakland, CA 94604

BBW (Big, Beautiful Woman)
9171 Wilshire Blvd., Suite 300
Beverly Hills, CA 90210

The Crossing Press
publishes many books of special interest to women.
For a current catalog, please call toll-free
1-800-777-1048.